The Best of

Us

A Spiritual Road Map for Parents

— Tim Ferguson —

WESTBOW
PRESS®
A DIVISION OF THOMAS NELSON
& ZONDERVAN

Scripture taken from the Holy Bible, NEW INTERNATIONAL VERSION®.
Copyright © 1973, 1978, 1984 by Biblica, Inc. All rights reserved worldwide.
Used by permission. NEW INTERNATIONAL VERSION® and NIV® are
registered trademarks of Biblica, Inc. Use of either trademark for the offering
of goods or services requires the prior written consent of Biblica US, Inc.

WestBow Press books may be ordered through booksellers or by contacting:

WestBow Press
A Division of Thomas Nelson & Zondervan
1663 Liberty Drive
Bloomington, IN 47403
www.westbowpress.com
1 (866) 928-1240

Because of the dynamic nature of the Internet, any web addresses or
links contained in this book may have changed since publication and
may no longer be valid. The views expressed in this work are solely those
of the author and do not necessarily reflect the views of the publisher,
and the publisher hereby disclaims any responsibility for them.

Any people depicted in stock imagery provided by Thinkstock are models,
and such images are being used for illustrative purposes only.
Certain stock imagery © Thinkstock.

ISBN: 978-1-5127-2247-5 (sc)
ISBN: 978-1-5127-2248-2 (hc)
ISBN: 978-1-5127-2272-7 (e)

Library of Congress Control Number: 2015919970

Print information available on the last page.

WestBow Press rev. date: 12/22/2015

CONTENTS

FOREWORD

"Few people have shaped my spiritual destiny like Pastor Tim Ferguson. Drawing from biblical wisdom and a wealth of life experience, Tim gives parents practical tools on how to raise children that will seek first the kingdom of God in the midst of a seek-yourself culture. If you've ever wished that your kids came with an instruction manual or just needed some direction in navigating the daunting waters of parenthood, then I highly recommend this book."

Robert Madu
Evangelist

ACKNOWLEDGEMENTS

To Jim and Becky Hennesy, thanks for being my pastor, my boss and my friend for the last twenty-one years. I could not have done this without your leadership.

To all my friends at Trinity Church, it has been an incredible journey with each of you. I love our time of working and worshipping together.

Thanks to Jorge Parrales, my editor. Your insights, encouragement and critiques have inspired me to be a better writer.

To Michelle's parents, Larry and Linda Click, when I was a youth pastor, I used to tell teenagers who were dating to *"never underestimate the power of good in-laws."* You are the best in-laws any husband could ever have. Thank you for always being there for us.

To Mom, Dad, Delisa, Cherie and Tami Jean. We are not an expressive family in words or outward displays of affection. But this book could not have been written without the memories of our shared lives together. There is a bond between us that only strong families can truly understand. I love each of you more than you can imagine.

To Michelle, my best friend, and the love of my life. Thank you for twenty-six years together as my parenting partner. Our journey has exceeded my wildest dreams. We will always have my favorite verse in Proverbs.

To Paul, David and Susanna. Words cannot express how proud I am of each of you. As you enter adulthood, my love for you grows deeper every day. You truly are **the best of us.**

INTRODUCTION

I still remember the cold, January day in Cedar Hill, Texas like it is a moment frozen in time. I was in the middle of basketball practice preparing my team for a big district game the following evening. I looked up for an instant and saw my beautiful wife, Michelle, walk into the gym. It was obvious by the look on her face that she had something important she wanted to tell me.

Understand, this is before cell phones, text messaging and social media allowed instant access into every detail of our lives. If you wanted to communicate with someone, unless they were sitting at home by their land line telephone, it had to be done face to face.

Most of you reading this right now are probably imagining the smile on my face as I saw her approach me. After all, it had only been six months since I pledged my eternal love for her before God and in front of all our family and friends. But you would be mistaken, because I did not smile and I definitely was not happy. If there was one thing I hated, it was being interrupted during the middle of practice.

Then she held up a tiny pair of Nike basketball shoes and a Texas Rangers baby bottle. My anger turned to confusion and after a few seconds my confusion melted into the realization of the meaning of those little shoes.

Michelle was pregnant. We were going to have a baby! My first thought was, "How could this have happened?" Followed quickly by, "I'm not qualified to be a parent. Shouldn't I be required to get some type of license first?" Do not misunderstand me, I know where babies come from and how they are made. But we had planned to wait three years until starting our family. *(Let me take a moment to warn new couples that if you have sex, you might get pregnant, regardless of the precautions you have taken.)*

Almost immediately statements full of contradictions began to come out of my mouth. "We can't afford a baby right now." "Boy or girl?" "Decorate the nursery in Dallas Cowboy or Texas Longhorn colors?" "We haven't been married long enough to have a child." The rush of emotions surprised me, because I had spent most of my adolescent and young adult years declaring my opposition to this institution we call parenthood and now, in an instant, I'm a dad. The words of Job came to my mind, ***"What I feared has come upon me; what I dreaded has happened to me." (Job 3:25)***

That January afternoon twenty-five years ago began a journey that still continues to this day. The baby boy who filled those basketball shoes has graduated from college with a pastoral ministries degree and is teaching Bible to junior high students in the same Christian school where I have coached and taught for most of my adult life.

Along the years we were blessed with two more children *(I really want to use the word "kids", but my boss once told me that a kid was a baby goat and even though my children often destroyed things like baby goats I will use the formal words for them throughout this book)* which added weight to our parenting responsibility. It would be idealistic to call being a parent the "greatest adventure," because it is often more like ABC's Wide World of Sports; "the thrill of victory and the agony of defeat." *(I realize that many of you have no idea what ABC's Wide World of Sports is, but there is a reason God gave us Google and YouTube.)*

I remember the joy and suffering (*actually, Michelle did all of the suffering*) of three pregnancies and the early infant stages. Because our children were born three years apart there was a toddler in the house for almost a decade. This meant I had to spend ten years of my life telling one of my children, "No, you can't watch Barney" or "Yes, Dad would love to eat some more pizza from Chuck E. Cheese's." Then there was pre-school and elementary, where the inadequacy of parenting raised its ugly head. It is at this stage that the comparison with other children gets intense. Their character and behavior flaws begin to be revealed and they are also judged by their academic prowess and athletic abilities. This is a difficult time for many parents, because our "faithful" excuses (*he's tired, she's not feeling very well or I think he/she is teething*) for our children's behavior do not work as well as they used to. From elementary it is on to junior high and high school where every successful decision for your child's first twelve years has now been rendered obsolete. The son or daughter you have grown to cherish and love is now only a distant memory (*more on this in Chapter 6*).

Michelle and I are currently traveling a road that involves a high school senior, a college student and a young adult who has just stepped out into the world. The parenting journey for us today is just as uncertain as it was when we first began way back in the 20th century.

As we approach this new stage of our lives, I have decided to write a book. You may ask, "Why write a book on parenting? Aren't there enough books already?" You're probably right. The world's wisest man once said **"There's nothing new under the sun." (Ecclesiastes 1:9)** But I am going to write it anyway. Why? One reason I'm typing words to screen is because writing a book is on my lifetime bucket list. It does not matter if anyone actually reads this book, because it is important to me that I accomplish this goal. (*I'm not being completely truthful. I really want everyone to buy this book so I will have enough money to pay for David and Susanna's college tuition.*) I also am writing this book because God has put some thoughts and ideas in my heart that might help someone. Mostly I'm writing this because talking about parenting struggles with others *(you)* is helping me deal with the radical change occurring in my emotions as my children near the time when I will cease to be their authority and will have to move into a role as their mentor and friend.

Another question you may be asking is, "How can it help me?" One of my goals is for this book to be as timeless as possible. Our first two children were born way back in a time when Al Gore had not yet invented the internet *(I just realized that by referencing Al Gore I have already dated my book as antiquated and all those born after 1995 should stop reading right now)*. The internet has become one of the biggest challenges every parent faces as they navigate the complexities of raising a child. When our children were born, only a few people in the military had ever even conceived of the possibility of the World Wide Web, much less how it would affect parenting. So how could anyone have given us a road map to help us with decisions regarding the internet? There will be something in your future as a parent that will be new, exciting and potentially dangerous to the spiritual well-being of your child.

This book is not a how-to-book. It is a book of spiritual, emotional and practical principles to help guide all those who daily deal with difficult parenting decisions. It is written to help parents who are just beginning their journey or who have years of experience. It is a book for blended families or single moms and dads, and for grandparents or close relatives who have been assigned the responsibility of guiding a child successfully along the path toward their God-given destiny.

There is some apprehension facing me as I undertake this assignment of imparting parenting principles to others. Even though our sons and daughter to this point have exceeded our desires regarding their faith, moral decisions, relationships and career pursuits, there is still a little voice whispering in my head, "You've only just begun to fight."

Many of life's most difficult decisions are still ahead of them. How will they handle these moments? Will adversity or disappointment over unfulfilled hopes and dreams send them traveling down a wrong road? How will I look to the readers of this book if my children do not look so perfect? *(Depending on the day, they don't always look so perfect to me now.)* These are not pleasant, happy thoughts, but these are the fears every parent faces along every stage of a child's development.

There is a core belief each of us should have regarding the goodness of God. No matter what circumstances we encounter on our parenting timelines I believe that the best is yet to come. This is my message to every parent. If you are a parent staring at an unknown future, the best is yet to come. If you are a parent going through a storm with your child, the best is yet to come. If you are a parent experiencing a season of favor over your child, something better is still to come.

That's my message and this is my story. I trust that these truths will breathe hope and peace into your hearts as you travel along life's parenting path.

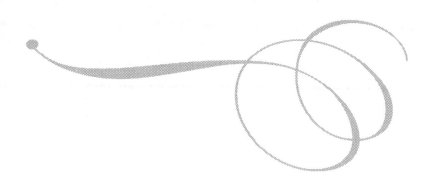

CHAPTER 1

The Best Is Yet To Come

"For I know the plans I have for you," declares the Lord, "plans to prosper you and not to harm you, plans to give you a hope and a future."
Jeremiah 29:11

"The best is yet to come and babe, won't it be fine?
The best is yet to come, come the day you're mine
Come the day you're mine
And you're gonna be mine"
Frank Sinatra - The Best Is Yet To Come

"Yes, your baby is dead, all right." Said the specialist, who was examining the grainy picture of the sonogram in front of him.

Only twenty-four hours earlier I had received another visit to the gym. This time it was during volleyball practice, again bringing me news regarding the pregnancy of my wife. I looked up from the drill we were running, but it was not Michelle standing in front of me, it was her mom. It was immediately evident something was wrong as my mother-in-law walked over to me and said that Michelle needed to see me outside.

As I approached the car I could tell that Michelle was crying and that something really bad had occurred. My first thought was that something had happened to Paul *(our oldest son, who was three at the time)*. But I remembered about the appointment with Dr. Tullar on our schedule earlier in the morning for the sixth month checkup of our twin boys, David and Daniel.

That's right, my wife was not only pregnant with another baby, but we were having twins. Seeing those sonogram images months ago for the first time, images that showed the life of two sons in her womb, had caused quite a shock. Shock at twice the work, twice the amount of money needed for diapers, clothes and formula *(don't judge me for the formula, I did my best to convince Michelle to breastfeed, even though my motives were more money related than health related)*. But after a few weeks, the shocking twin discovery turned into an excitement that I was soon going to be the father of three boys. I was well on my way to my own basketball team, or at the very least, we had a complete golf foursome.

At the car that day all of those dreams came crashing to a halt as through tears she informed me Dr. Tullar had said the sonogram was showing that Daniel did not have any signs of life. Thinking back on that day now over two decades later, the pain of that revelation still carries quite a punch. There is the guilt I feel for not being there at the doctor's office when Michelle received the news, and there is still a little anger at God for allowing us to go through such devastating trial.

Dr. Tullar, our obstetrician, scheduled an appointment the following day with a specialist who he said would be able to give us answers to all the heartbroken questions running through our minds. The next day's appointment was the moment when the sonogram specialist confirmed our worst fears when he told us that Dr. Tullar's initial diagnosis had been correct.

He informed us of all the dangers still facing David, who remained alive in Michelle's womb and finished his meeting with us by saying if our remaining son was born alive, he would probably be brain-damaged. We left his office and headed to the parking lot with Michelle sobbing almost uncontrollably. In the front seat of our car we just sat there in stunned silence, not knowing what to do or say for what seemed like hours.

All of a sudden, I felt a faith arise in my soul. It was the gift of faith I had read about many times in 1 Corinthians chapter 12 but had never experienced personally before. Being raised in a Pentecostal home meant that I believed in miracles and had seen many people ask God for some great healing, but I had never had a situation in my life that needed a miracle of this magnitude. I turned to Michelle and held her close and I remember these words coming out of my mouth: "We can let Daniel go and give him to the Lord or we can begin to believe God for a miracle...a miracle that will raise Daniel from the dead inside the womb ...a miracle to see David born alive and healthy with no complications."

It seems crazy, right? Who in their right mind prays for a dead baby in the womb to live? But we had moved out of natural and we had moved into believing for something miraculous. In spite of the overwhelming circumstances facing us over the next two to three months of Michelle's pregnancy, we truly began to believe that the best was yet to come.

Believing in a preferable future over your children is not just some words we recite to ourselves or a mental game we play when the fears begin to overtake our minds. Believing the best is yet to come is taking hold of God's promise of a future and a hope over our sons and daughters.

God reminded me that he had given us a promise over our home and a specific promise for each of our children. For Paul, it was the assurance from the psalmist that **goodness and mercy would follow (him) all the days of his life (Psalm 23:6).** For David and Daniel, the word over them was where the Bible revealed to us that children were **a heritage from the Lord, children a reward from him *(Psalm 127:3).*** It was through this chapter that freedom from financial fear came, when I read a dad is blessed when his arrow quiver is full of children. It was this passage that declared we would never be ashamed of David when he fights the enemy at the gates of Hades. When fear and doubt rise against you, when the pain and devastation of loss comes in like a flood, then only the Word of God spoken over your home, your family, and your children will be able to sustain you.

My friends, Robert and Taylor, recently gave birth to a beautiful baby girl. I asked Robert about the emotions he felt when he held Evie for the first time. His reply: "She was beauty and innocence defined. A part of me is in my arms, the future is bright and all my desires are wrapped up in this little blanket. But then doubt and waves of fear began to fill my mind." Within seconds of one of the greatest days of his life, his hopes for his daughter were already under attack.

This is the spiritual battle every parent faces daily. Those doubts, those fears are from the enemy of our soul. He is devising a strategy to destroy the destiny of our children even as we are decorating the nursery and deciding the exact details of their seventeen year educational journey. The only effective way to combat these attacks is to rest on the promise that God has also planned out the best for our children because his strategy is for their good, not for evil. According to King David in Psalm 139, God's strategy was conceived even while our sons and daughters were in the womb. Before they were even a twinkle in our eyes, or a thought in our mind, God had already predestined them for greatness.

On a dark day outside the doctor's office many years ago, a spiritual lesson was imprinted on my heart and mind. If I was going to believe the best was yet to come over David and Daniel, then fear had to be driven from my spirit. The Holy Spirit proceeded to fill my thoughts with faith verses from the Bible that I had memorized as boy in Sunday school *(This was an ancient religious activity from a forgotten time used by parents to teach stories and verses from the Bible to their children).* Scripture drove out fear and I began to believe again in the God of the impossible.

NO FEAR

When the Apostle Paul sat down to pen his last letter to the New Testament church, it was not written to the Church at Rome or to a group of people in Asia Minor. He wrote a personal letter, a letter to his spiritual son, Timothy. This epistle was designed to inspire his son to continue in the faith, to help him remember the spiritual gifts that God had deposited inside of him, and to encourage Timothy to overcome all the obstacles the enemy had placed before him. Paul was in a Roman prison, awaiting execution for his faith in Jesus. How did he spend his last moments on this earth? By talking to his son, telling him that in spite of the circumstances, the best is yet to come. Paul started this letter by addressing the one giant blocking Timothy's future. What was holding Timothy back? It was fear. He had a fear of the unknown, a fear of being too young, a fear of not being qualified. Paul softly rebuked him at the beginning of the letter as he asked Timothy to remember his call and his purpose. Then Paul wrote the following encouraging words to his young disciple; ***For God has not given us a spirit of fear, but of power and of love and of a sound mind (2 Timothy 1:7 NKJV).***

Fear is not a gift from God. God wants us to walk through life with no fear. Do you remember the No Fear t-shirt company that exploded on the national scene a few years ago? They contained inspirational phrases like:

> *"World Series, 2 outs, bottom of the 9th, bases loaded, down 3, 3-2 pitch...No Fear."*

> *"I've never lost, I've just been a little behind when time expired...No Fear."*

These t-shirts were designed to inspire greatness in the lives of the modern sports participants. The main point of these shirts was to remind the athletes and those reading the motivational slogans that it is impossible to succeed in the arena of sports if the athlete is afraid of the moment of opportunity. In the same way, it is impossible for parents to create a championship environment for their children if they are paralyzed by fear.

Paul's message to his son Timothy gives us an effective blueprint to combat fear. This truth simply says "fear is not from God." Long before No Fear shirts were invented, Paul told his readers that when they were in a battle for spiritual destiny to have no fear. The fear described here comes from the Greek word, deilia, which literally means, "to be a coward." This word is never used in a good light in the Bible. This type of fear is not from God.

I am aware that there is another meaning for fear in God's Word. Solomon said ***"The fear of the Lord is the beginning of knowledge." (Proverbs 1:7)*** The New Testament describes this type of fear by telling us ***that those who want to worship God should worship Him with fear and awe (Hebrews 12:28).*** This fear is a reverence. It is a respect for the power of something that is greater than we are. It is a sense of awe that causes us to take shelter from a tornado or to flee inland from the path of a hurricane. This reverent fear is a healthy part of our everyday lives and is a useful tool in helping our children make good decisions. We tell our young children, "no playing in the street," because we know that the power of the automobile is stronger than our child's body. It is not cowardly fear to tell this to a two year old because they are unable to mentally process the danger at such a young age. But if you are still telling your twenty-one year old young adult son to "look both ways before crossing the street," then destructive fear, a spirit of fear not from God, may be operating in your life.

This is the type of fear Paul is addressing to Timothy. It is a fear that is causing him to be timid, a fear that results in being intimidated by the circumstances surrounding him. When it comes to your children, do not allow this destructive fear to invade your spirit. Most parents in my relational circle spend most of their child development strategy based on anything they feel is a threat to their child's well-being. We are afraid of our infant children choking, getting a deadly disease from the church's nursery or dying in their sleep from SIDS. As our children get older our concerns regarding their safety can range from eating too much refined sugar, getting lost at big events or even the danger of being kidnapped by a sexual predator. The problem with cowardly fear is there is never a pause or off button to push that allows a parent to breathe easily. This fear always haunts our minds because even as they become the young men and women we aspire for them to be, there are still parent panic attacks at the possibility of car wrecks and broken hearts from unrequited love.

What I like most about Paul's instructions to Timothy about fear is that he gave us a spiritual blueprint; an outline of how to defeat fear. Do you want to walk in the spirit of no fear? Do you want to defeat the anxiety attacks over your child's future and be able to believe that the best is yet to come? Then listen and respond to what Paul has to say.

FEAR

...m on high, a power as described by Paul here in this verse, is a power that has the ability to drive out all fear. Many of you know the Greek word for power in the New Testament is the word, dunamis, from which is derived the English word, "dynamite." If we will access this power, the same power that **raised Jesus from the dead (Romans 8:11)**, then many nights of peaceful rest will be available to you. Countless times over the years I have accessed this spiritual dynamite over fears relating to our children, and God has never let me down.

One of the biggest challenges in our marriage over the years has been this struggle Michelle and I have concerning the physical safety of our children. I grew up in rural East Texas and spent much of my free time during my childhood testing the limits of the guardian angels assigned by God to protect me. Michelle, on the other hand, sees danger lurking around every corner as she thinks all of Hades is poised to pounce on our offspring *(if you think I am not being very kind to my wife, keep in mind I have my own spiritual issues, like anger, that the Lord uses to keep me humble).* So you can understand the heated discussions we occasionally have anytime I come up with an idea that might put one of our children's potential well-being at risk.

Our oldest son Paul was only nine when I convinced Michelle to allow him to travel with me to the Czech Republic for our summer youth missions trip. We flew into the city of Prague, which in my opinion is one of the most romantic cities in the world *(Charles River Bridge at night).* From Prague, we traveled to Podborany, a small city in northern Czech, where we would spend the week holding outreach services to the local community. As soon as we arrived in the city our team was given the responsibility for setting up the meeting tent, the stage and sound system. During our set up I looked around to see Paul playing Olympic long jump from wooden stage platform to platform. Immediately I could tell that this activity was potentially dangerous to his health and because I remembered

Michelle's warning (*"if anything happens to my son over there, I'll never forgive you"*), I may have raised my voice at my young son to tell him to stop jumping.

But as our children are apt to do, he obeyed for a while and as soon as I turned my back he resumed his Evel Knievel activity. I am sure you can probably see where this story is heading. A few minutes later I heard an anguished scream so I turned to see Paul pick himself up off the ground next to a platform and grab his leg as he headed straight toward me crying. My memories of the moments that followed are clouded with the passage of time, but I do recall saying, "I told you to stop jumping, get over there and sit down until I tell you to get up!" My firstborn son hobbled over to the metal folding chair and proceeded to pull up his sweats to check his injury. Watching from across the tent I was still filled with righteous anger at his disobedience of my command *(compassion is not always my strong suit)*. He pulled up his pants leg and what I saw took my breath away while filling me with an ocean of fear. Paul had a long, deep cut on the front part of his leg just below his right knee. When he attempted the last jump he had fallen a bit short and hit the edge of the wooden platform with his shin. He was bleeding and I could see his white bone through the flesh even though I was about thirty yards away. I raced over to him, took off my t-shirt, wrapped it tightly around his open wound and started crying out for someone to call for medical help.

I do not know if I can adequately describe the cascade of emotions I faced in the minutes that followed. "Will he bleed to death? Could he lose his leg? What's Michelle going to say when she finds out?" Keep in mind, we are in a small town in the Czech Republic and I have no idea what medical doctors or facilities are available. I did what any of you would do when faced with a life-threatening challenge over the life of your son. I started to pray. No, I mean really praying, not a soft prayer, but a loud prayer of desperation. The longer we waited the more I prayed, and the more I prayed, the more the fears seemed to fade. Then I felt the voice of the Holy Spirit say, "No fear, I've got your back. Paul is going to be fine."

The Holy Spirit was right. Paul would be fine. The power of God to heal my son was greater than all my fears. The bleeding was miraculously kept to a minimum, he had no broken bones, the medical attention we received in that small Czech town was remarkable and Michelle did forgive me for putting our son's life at risk. Every now and then, when he is wearing shorts, I will notice the big Nike looking scar on his leg and am again reminded at the faithfulness of a powerful God.

The Bible is full of illustrative stories of God's power triumphing over natural fear. Nebuchadnezzar used this intimidation tactic when he said **"What God will be able to rescue you from my hand?" (Daniel 3:15)** to Hananiah, Meshael and Azariah after they refused to bow to the golden idol (*I know most of you think of them by their Babylonian names, but I think they are in heaven today shouting, "Don't call us Shadrach, Meshach and Abednego."*). But in the midst of the fire, Jesus would show up and His power would defeat the flames and the fear of death.

Pharaoh tried the same strategy during the Israelites' exodus when he led his chariot army out of Egypt and trapped Moses and the children of Israel up against the Red Sea. But Moses knew his help came from The Lord. He had seen the dynamite power of God who had delivered them from slavery with the miracle of the ten plagues. He was not intimidated by the enemy and as a result he stretched out his hand with his rod and saw the parting of the Red Sea and the destruction of Pharaoh's army. Do not shrink back from the enemy. Go on attack against the Nebuchadnezzars and Pharaohs who try to bring destruction to your sons and daughters. When my son Paul was in trouble in Czech, I did not give in to fear. I called on the power of God and he delivered me.

We have access to this power through the Holy Spirit. It is a power to heal, a power to see miracles and a power to break the stronghold of fear over your mind. God's power is greater than the enemy's fear. But there is also another weapon promised to us from the Apostle Paul found in 2 Timothy 1.

LOVE > FEAR

In March of 2003 I had just completed a round at the Pebble Beach Golf Course in Northern California. If you enjoy playing golf then Pebble Beach is on the short list of courses that you dream of playing before your time on earth is finished. My friend Chris and I made our way back to our hotel room for one last night on the majestic Pacific Ocean before we headed home to resume our normal lives. We turned on the television and were jolted back to reality as we watched the United States launch a full scale bombing attack on the nation of Iraq.

The situation was a little disconcerting for me because this was only eighteen months since the terrorist attacks on September 11, 2001. Flying on a plane the day after we went to war with another nation seemed to be a little dangerous. But if I was somewhat nervous, my friend Chris was petrified with fear. He wrestled with the fear of his physical safety versus the business responsibilities he had back home before coming up with a workable solution. You see, I was traveling home on Southwest Airlines making a couple of stops along the way while Chris was flying non-stop business class on American Airlines. His plan to conquer his fear of being blown out of the sky by terrorists was to buy me a business class ticket next to him on his flight. I asked him why he would make such an expensive purchase just to have me as company on his flight. He replied, "You're a pastor. I know God loves you and he won't let anything happen to our plane with you on it." Without even realizing it my friend had discovered one of the great truths in defeating fear. **There is no fear in love. But perfect love drives out fear (1 John 4:18).**

If we could only understand that God's perfect unconditional love for our children is so much more than the natural parental love we have for them, it would change our perspective. God loves our sons and daughters and will not allow them to suffer, be hurt or be tempted beyond what they can bear. If you can believe in the "agape" love from your children's Heavenly Father then you will be able to find the ***peace of God that transcends all understanding (Philippians 4:7).***

As I write this chapter it is important for you to know that these statements are not just empty words. What I am writing has to be "spirit and life" to me since I am facing one of the most difficult trials of my life. Michelle just called saying my younger sister Tami received a report from the doctor that her breast cancer has returned and is in the bone of her sternum. Words like metastatic, incurable and Stage IV bring an intimidating assault on my faith. What am I feeling? "She's too young. What about my eleven and eight year old nephews? God, what about all those promises of your healing power? Why am I even writing this stupid book?" I am thirteen years older than my sister and as an older brother I feel the same way toward her as I do toward my own children. But today, I rest in God's Word. The love I know God has for my sister, who has served him all her life, drives out my fear and I start believing again that the best is yet to come for her and for her family.

God's power is greater than my fear and God's love is stronger than my doubt. I choose to trust in his faithfulness and his word. There is one last weapon found in Paul's message to Timothy.

A SOUND MIND > FEAR

One of my favorite narratives from the life of Jesus is found in the book of Mark. John Mark, an author of one of the four gospels, does not spend any time on Old Testament prophecies, boring genealogies or "Away in a Manger" stories about the baby Jesus. No, he skips right to the adult Jesus and his earthly ministry beginning with his baptism by his cousin John. By the time we start reading chapter 3 Jesus has already driven out evil spirits, healed a leper and said "rise and walk" to a paralyzed man lowered through the roof of a house. Large crowds have begun to follow Jesus and ministry controversy has risen regarding the lifestyle of his disciples and his apparent violation of the Sabbath laws.

When the news of Jesus' rock star status reached his mother and his brothers, they traveled to Capernaum, which is about forty miles from Jesus' hometown of Nazareth. Did Mary travel all those miles on foot just to spend quality time with her son? No. She came to Jesus because she thought he was *"out of his mind." (Mark 3:21)* His brothers came with their mom so they could physically take their older brother away to a first century mental institution.

They believed Jesus was not in his right mind, but the reality of the situation is that his family had allowed fear to penetrate their spirit and to affect the decisions they were making. Mary had been visited by Gabriel, given birth through a supernatural encounter with the Holy Spirit and had experienced all the miracles of the Christmas story. Yet here she is thirty years later bound by fear over whether or not the best was yet to come for her son. The promises and prophecies of those early years felt so far way. All her faith was gone and fear was causing Mary to make decisions that were not of a sound mind.

I have always found Paul's last piece of advice regarding combating fear in this verse confusing. What does having a sound mind actually mean? Other Bible translations describe this as self-control, self-discipline, or being sober. It makes me want to tell the Apostle Paul, "That's not much of a news flash. I know I need self-control. If I had self-control then I wouldn't be struggling with fear." But suddenly it was like a light bulb was turned on in my negative thinking. I was reminded of the fruits of the Spirit listed in Galatians and how the last of the nine fruits listed was self-control. If the

Holy Spirit gives us dynamite power and a revelation of his perfect love, then he also gives us the ability to have self-discipline over our emotions in the middle of dark trials and tribulations.

God wants us to have a sound mind because fear is like drinking too much alcohol. A man who is physically drunk will make bad, dangerous decisions that can affect his future for years. Fear over the future of your children will result in you making drunken choices over the details of their lives. Do you spend most of your waking hours imagining the worst possible outcomes over your sons and daughters? Do you replay negative comments spoken by others about your children over and over again in your mind? If so, then you are drunk with fear and you need God to give you self-control and self-discipline. A sound mind that is led by the Spirit triumphs over the enemy when it comes to the direction of your child's future.

Our story of David and Daniel's birth required a decision to walk with this sound mind instead of fear. This was absolutely necessary because the days that followed the news of the apparent death of our Daniel were marked by a strong temptation to doubt that God's best was at work on our behalf.

Michelle would almost immediately go into premature labor and spent the entire rest of her pregnancy in bed. This resulted in Michelle being hooked up to an experimental Tokos Contraction Monitor at a cost of over one thousand dollars a day. It went from bad to worse for us when our insurance company said that they would not cover this life saving monitor recommended by our doctor. We turned to our spiritual family for support during this difficult trial. But surprisingly, some people whom we thought would believe with us for a miracle instead described to us in detail some horrific infant death story. Others tried to spiritualize the reason behind the loss of our son. Fear was attacking us every minute and every hour for almost seventy days. The attacks were on our faith, our finances, Michelle's health and the life of our sons.

How did we fight this fear from the pits of Hades? There were two important ingredients to being able to overcome the enemy's schemes and tactics. First, in the midst of our trial we had a few close friends and family members who believed for the impossible and constantly reminded us that God's best was still ahead. Secondly, we were given self-control, a sound mind, from the Holy Spirit which allowed us to make decisions about the pregnancy with God's wisdom and not man's opinion or common sense.

The title of this chapter is The Best Is Yet to Come. So if Paul Harvey *(my dad always loved Paul Harvey)* was still alive he would give you "the rest of the story." But he is no longer with us so I guess it falls to me to finish our story regarding the birth of our twin sons.

After over two months of being bedridden, the doctors believed Michelle was far enough along in the pregnancy to be able to safely give birth. So they removed her from the monitor and all the drugs she had been taking to keep her from going into premature labor. Within hours after these actions were implemented, Michelle began experiencing intense contractions and we found ourselves on the way to the hospital for the moment of truth.

The labor and delivery room experience was so much different than when Paul was born. Only three years earlier we were accompanied in our hospital room by our nurse while Dr. Tullar occasionally came in to check on her progress until it was time for the actual birth. This time everything was not quite so calm and relaxed. There were doctors, nurses and emergency equipment all around the room. I knew that her labor was still a month too early, but I was not prepared for all the activity around Michelle that was foreshadowing a potential medical crisis. For an instant, my faith left me and fear started to take a hold of my spirit. But the Vineyard worship music playing in the room brought a peace that allowed me to know God had everything under control.

David was born first. He was alive and healthy at a robust six pounds. In spite of all the concerns, there were no complications and we were able to take him home the next day. Daniel came next. He was not alive. The sting of death had shriveled his once beautifully formed body into only a few pounds of unrecognizable flesh. All of our prayers, all of our faith had failed. God did not show up with a miracle. But there was a peace from God in the room that truly was "beyond all human understanding." Michelle and I prayed over the little broken body of our third son and gave him back to God. After a few more moments with Michelle, I left the room to give the news to our family and friends. As I walked down the hall with Dr. Tullar, he put his arm around me and said he had something to tell me that he had never told me before. The following words sent a holy chill down my back: "Michelle's situation was outside our expertise so I sent her blood work to the Mayo Clinic. What we now know is this. A blood vessel in Daniel ruptured and bled into Michelle's blood and caused a poisoning that flowed back into Daniel's body. But what we can't understand is how it didn't kill Michelle or David. Your wife and son are a walking miracle."

God did hear our prayers. The miracle we prayed for would ultimately be different than our earthly expectations. Every year on David's birthday, I take some time to offer thanks to God for answering our prayers. I will go to my grave believing our decision to walk by faith, to walk with no fear, had opened the windows of heaven so that a physical miracle would be available for Michelle and David. I also know that our son Daniel awaits us in heavenly places and someday we will all worship the Lord together. God did not stop there. Our trial awakened in us an understanding that our heavenly Father truly had a plan and a purpose over our family regarding every detail of our lives. There was one final miracle as a few days later we received a call from the Tokos Medical Corporation, telling us they had some good news regarding our insurance company's refusal to pay for the contractions monitor. The representative told me they had decided to wave our $70,000 bill because we had been through enough pain. The financial favor could not negate the pain over Daniel's death, but it did let us know God was still watching out for us.

Most of what I believe about being a parent was forged out of this season of our lives. When times get tough, when fear sweeps in, I am reminded of God's faithfulness during our darkest hour. I remember his peace. I remember the financial and physical miracles and once again I start to believe God's promises over my family that the best is yet to come. The spiritual truths that are to come in the following chapters are designed to guide you on the most difficult journey of your life; the spiritual journey of seeing God's best be fulfilled in the lives of those you love the most. Let these words be "spirit and life" to your parenting soul.

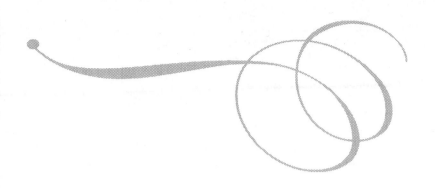

CHAPTER 2

SEE THE BEST

"Now faith is being sure of what we hope for and certain of what we do not see."

Hebrews 11:1

"See your future. Be...your future. May...make...make it. Make it! Make your future...Danny."

Ty Webb - Caddyshack

"Human Video Solo, David Ferguson, a score of excellent." Those words drove a dagger into my soul as I felt the crushing weight of disappointment that only comes when all hope has been lost.

The setting for this day of parenting defeat was at our denomination's District Fine Arts competition *(the best way to describe the intensity of fine arts would be for you to imagine a large regional youth cheerleading or gymnastics tournament on steroids).* In North Texas, over one thousand students in junior high and high school come together to compete in various art, drama and musical categories. All of these teenagers perform before a panel of three judges in a solo or group event attempting to score high enough to advance to nationals, where thousands of students from all over the nation would converge in Orlando, Florida later that year.

For most of his life, David had watched Fine Arts through the lens of a pastor's son as he traveled to these competitions each year because Michelle and I had the responsibility of overseeing all the students participating. David had always dreamed of the day when he would be old enough to win trophies, scholarships and personal accolades in drama, short sermon, and human video categories. I realize that most of you reading this have no idea what a human video is *(a five to seven minute Christian drama, usually a story from the Bible set to music...think Michael Jackson's Thriller),* and even if you did, I am sure you would be wondering why anyone would ever think this was an organized activity worth pursuing. But strangely enough, the human video category is by far the most popular event at the district and national level; at nationals, if your large human video group makes it to the final round, there is a crowd participation and excitement that can only be compared to a Friday night lights football game.

Now David's day had finally arrived and he believed that it was now his time to shine. His excitement at the opportunity to compete for the first time resulted in what I thought was an unrealistic expectation of fine arts success. His faith in his dramatic abilities resulted in his participation in seven categories for his seventh grade year. In his mind, hundreds and thousands of students would soon be chanting his name as he led his church youth group to fine arts glory.

I, on the other hand, approached his first year with great fear and trepidation. The reason? I knew something about David that he had yet to discover about himself. He had very little talent or aptitude *(or so my logical, fact-driven mind told me)* for anything related to fine arts. In my educated opinion *(youth pastor with years of fine arts experience)* he could not act, carry a tune, play an instrument and was probably the worst teenage public speaker I had ever coached. Watching my son believe for greatness, spend hours practicing and put his heart and soul into his performances only to be a witness to his failure that weekend was like observing a car wreck in slow motion over and over again. Seven times his name was called and seven times a score of excellent *("excellent" in fine arts signifies failure because it means you are not good enough to advance to nationals)* was read aloud to all the students. When it was all said and done, David was the only person in our youth group *(around 100 students)* that day who did not advance to nationals in at least one category. I looked for him so I could offer some comfort and consolation but quickly realized that he had disappeared from the room. After several minutes of searching I finally found him locked in a bathroom stall crying over the humiliation of such an unforeseen outcome.

I cannot adequately describe the heartbreak and pain I felt at seeing my son fail. No words of "You did your best" or "I'm proud of you for giving your all" were going to be sufficient for this moment. I could hear the enemy whispering in my spiritual ears, "Your son is destined for failure. I will always be here to crush his hopes and dreams." These are critical moments in the lives of every parent. It is the realization that all of our parenting skills and expertise cannot make life better for our sons and daughters when they encounter life's inevitable cruelty. How will you respond when the path to their promised future appears to be blocked by the facts? The answer is simple. When the adversary releases all of his forces against your children, when he whispers death's dark promise over your child's emotional and spiritual well-being, when he places an emotional fog over your spiritual eyes regarding their destiny...See the best.

WHAT DO YOU SEE?

What is faith? *Faith is being sure of what we hope for and certain of what we do not see (Hebrews 11:1).* Or as my dad used to say, "If you can see it, it ain't faith."

I feel extremely unqualified to write this chapter because one of the greatest challenges I face in my spiritual journey is my inclination to "see the facts" and not to see the best. In Star Wars terms, I am much more comfortable with the "dark side" of life than the "light". The "dark side" seems practical, logical and full of common sense while the "light" appears impossible, out of reach and a fantasy. As an avid sports fan I have found that it is much better for me emotionally to believe that my team is going to lose *(especially as a Dallas Cowboy fan)* every game they play. This makes perfect sense if you think about it. If they lose, I am not surprised or disappointed because I have already prepared myself mentally for their failure, but if my teams achieve the impossible and are victorious, then I can celebrate their unexpected success. It is a "no lose" way of thinking. The problem with my "just the facts" outlook on life is that it pushes its way into my spirit when it comes to seeing the best regarding the lives of my children. My tendency is to see their future based on what I have observed in the day-to-day details of their lives and not on the prophetic promises of God. But every parent who is a believer, who is a follower of Christ, has an obligation to see their child's destiny with spiritual eyes. If we choose to see their future based on the opinions of others or the wisdom of the world, then a door in the spirit realm is opened to their defeat. It is imperative that you see God's best over the lives of your children.

"Dark side" thinking is destructive. It is like the twelve spies sent by Moses into the land of Canaan. God tells Moses to send one leader from each of the tribes of Israel into the Promised Land to obtain the following information; ***"See what the land is like and whether the people who live there are strong or weak, few or many. What kind of land do they live in? Is it good or bad? What kind of towns do they live in? Are they unwalled or fortified? How is the soil? Is it fertile or poor? Are there trees on it or not? Do your best to bring back some of the fruit of the land." (Numbers 13:16-20)*** I have always had a problem understanding why God has Moses do this. He already knows what the land is like and it does not matter if the people are strong or weak or if their walls are fortified, because he had already promised Moses victory over the Canaanites back when he first called him to greatness *(Exodus 3:17)*. But I think I have the answer. God wanted to test the spiritual eyes of all the leaders before they entered the battle. He wanted to know "what they saw" when confronted with the overwhelming task that lay ahead of them.

Ten of the twelve spies returned telling tales about the great giants in the land and how they would be physically unable to defeat such a powerful army. When they looked at the impossible task in front of them all they could see were the "facts." They had what I like to call "grasshopper eyes." After the men returned, the "dark side" spies gave this report to Moses; ***"We saw the Nephilim (giants) there...we seemed like grasshoppers in our eyes, and we looked the same to them" (Numbers 13:33).***

When it comes to my children and their future greatness, I really have to battle this negative thinking. If my vision begins to look through the "eyes of a grasshopper" I immediately begin to remind myself of the names of the ten loser spies. Do you recognize the names of these "great" leaders from the tribes of Israel? Names like Shammua, Shaphat, Igal, Palti, Gaddiel, Gaddi, Ammiel, Sethur, Nahbi or Geuel. You likely have never heard of them. How about Joshua or Caleb? These are the names of all twelve spies sent into the land. The challenge they faced almost 3500 years ago is the same challenge each parent faces over the potential greatness that lies ahead of their children today.

"What Do You See?" Joshua and Caleb were giant-killers. With their eyes, they saw God's promises being fulfilled; with their eyes they, saw a future where they would defeat giants and take possession of the land; with their eyes, they only saw the good of the land and its unlimited possibilities. The other ten guys, well, they had "grasshopper eyes." With their eyes, they only saw giants and the fortified cities; with their eyes, they saw only problems and all the things that could go wrong; with their eyes, they only saw death and defeat. You do not want to go down in history like the ten "grasshoppers." No one remembers them, no one names their kids Igal or Palti. Even spell check gives me a red line every time I type one of their names. On the other hand, all of history remembers Joshua and Caleb. There are young men and boys all around us still bearing the name legacy of these two individuals who saw future greatness and not future failure with their spiritual eyes. When I am reminded of Joshua and Caleb, I shake off the "dark side" thinking and put on my spiritual glasses. My children, Paul, David and Susanna need a dad that sees their future through "giant-killer" eyes and not the eyes of a "grasshopper." Time and time again we read about the men and women who walked with God with a vision that impacted eternity. There are some things we can learn from what they saw that can help us with our parenting problems today,

WHAT YOU SEE IS OFTEN A MYSTICAL EXPERIENCE

In Scripture, whenever the heroes of our faith were searching for direction or guidance about their future, God would quite often reveal it through some mysterious, strange vision. Genesis

15 describes God confirming his promise of a son to Abraham by appearing as a smoking, fiery pot, as he passed between the pieces of animals that had been cut in half. This event is not some isolated occurrence. Jacob received his prophetic word from God at Bethel when he dreamed about angels in heaven going up and down a ladder. Joseph saw the sun, moon and stars bow down to him as God revealed a glimpse of his future in Egypt. Moses saw God as a burning bush in the wilderness, Joshua met the Captain of the Lord's army on the road to Jericho, and nobody had more strange prophetic visions about the future than the prophet Daniel.

Lest you think this spooky stuff is just Old Testament theology, remember it is the angel Gabriel who shows up in a teenage girl's bedroom to declare a virgin birth over her future. Peter followed Jesus after a miraculous catch of fish *(He knew if Jesus could see fish in the depths of the deep water then he could see into the sin hidden inside his heart.)* Philip is sent by the Holy Spirit alone into the desert to meet an Ethiopian, Paul is blinded on the road to Damascus and John has these weird revelations while exiled on the Isle of Patmos.

Maybe you are asking, "What's the point of these narratives from the Bible?" How does this relate to my struggles and concerns as a parent? I'm glad you asked. If you are going to be able to navigate this parenting journey successfully then you are going to need a vision from God regarding your child's future. Why do you need a mysterious experience from God? It is because almost as soon as your child is born, people begin to come out of the woodworks to give you their vision of your child's future. Comments like, "Oh, you're having a baby, get ready to worry about them for the rest of your life. Enjoy your peaceful child now, because the terrible two's are coming. Just wait until your kids are teenagers, they'll rebel against you and God." You must have a vision of a preferred future from God in regards to your children in order to survive spiritually and emotionally as a parent. King Solomon would give the best parenting advice ever when he said, ***"Where there is no vision, the people perish." (Proverbs 29:18 KJV)***

When Michelle and I started dating, we began a tradition each October to go on a date to the State Fair of Texas. The fair is everything that is good and right with the world. At the fair, you can dream of owning a car you will probably never be able to afford; at the fair, you can be convinced that if you buy this $500 set of steak knives, your life will be forever changed for the good; and at the fair, you can eat Fletcher's Corn Dogs, powdered sugar funnel cakes, and any fried desert you can imagine without gaining one extra pound. The State Fair grew into a family tradition over the years as we included our children and other various members of our extended family.

One beautiful October day, when our children were young and full of innocence *(they still showed us outward signs of affection)* we headed out to Fair Park near downtown Dallas for our annual descent into decadence. On this particular occasion, our daughter Susanna *(my princess)* had just turned two years old and was getting ready to experience her first fair day outside of a four-wheeled baby buggy.

As was our custom, the first thing we did on arrival was to head to the food court to begin our family time with a meal together. The food court at the State Fair is about the size of a football field with about eight exits. Our family *(about 20 of us)* grabbed a table and most began to explore the various booths of authentic Texas cuisine being offered at inflated prices around the building. I was about to head to the food station offering the chicken nachos and fried snickers bar with ice cream when Michelle asked me to stay at the table and watch Susanna while she made her food selection first. I sat down at the large table with Susanna to my right and my mom to my left and waited patiently *(actually, I was wondering why the husband always had to be stuck with babysitting duty on the fun trips)* for Michelle to return. My mom asked me a question and I turned my head away from Susanna to respond and when I turned my attention back to my young daughter a few moments later, she was gone. I immediately began to panic. People were everywhere and Susanna was nowhere to be seen. The State Fair feels safe during the day, but there were so many people and the location is not in the most secure area in the city of Dallas.

One minute of searching turned to two, and by the time Michelle and other family members arrived back at the table, a full-scale panic had settled into our hearts. Now it had been five minutes and I started thinking of every child kidnapping story I had ever read about or watched on television. We ran into friends from our church and they also began to look for Susanna. Just as I was about to head to the police station at the fair, I saw my friend, Misty Glover, heading towards me with Susanna in her arms. In the brief instant that my attention had been diverted she had made a bolt for freedom and headed out the back of the food court over one hundred yards away. This two year old girl walked out the building by herself onto the Midway where an elderly gentleman noticed her and picked her up to take her back inside to find her parents. Misty came out the door as the man was bringing Susanna back in the door and the rest, as you might say, is history. That night as I tried to go to sleep, I was still dealing with the emotional trauma of the near tragedy we had averted earlier in the day. The "grasshopper eyes" returned and I began to imagine how life could go wrong for my daughter as she grew older. But in the midst of the worst case scenario movie I was playing in my mind, I suddenly had what can only be described as a vision. Instead of the elderly man at the fair picking up my daughter in his arms so he could go find her parents, I saw Jesus wrap his arms around Susanna and carry her to safety. A word from David, the shepherd boy, came into my spirit as I heard The Lord say, ***"When the day of trouble comes I will keep Susanna safe...I will hide her in the shelter of My Presence and take her to a place of safety." (Psalm 27:5)*** In the stillness of the night I now knew that Susanna's future was in God's hands and he was always going to keep watch over my little girl. That vision gave me a peace and allowed me to once again see God's faithfulness over the lives of my children. Every parent needs a mystical vision from the throne of heaven to give them direction along life's parenting road.

WHAT YOU SEE SHOULD BE ETERNAL

There is a great scene in the Old Testament where God shows up to Abram *(soon to be called Abraham)* for the first time. Abraham is minding his own business living in Haran with his family. There is no record of a relationship between Abraham and God up until this time in Scripture. God gets right down to the point and begins to give Abraham life changing orders: *"Leave your country, your people and your father's household and go to the land I will show you." (Genesis 12:1)* One thing I like about following God is he does not just give us direction without a purpose. He follows the commands to Abraham with a promise. *"I will make you into a great nation and I will bless you: I will make your name great and you will be a blessing. I will bless those who bless you and whoever curses you I will curse; and all peoples on earth will be blessed through you." (Genesis 12:2-3)* Sometimes when we are familiar with a story we lose the impact of how difficult these decisions were for the people involved. In our minds all we hear is God's promise of greatness, instead of considering the cost of what God was really asking Abraham to do. Can you imagine his conversation with his wife Sarah following these instructions from God?

Abraham	*"God just told me that we are to leave my job, our home, all of our family and friends and go to a new place."*
Sarah	*"What did this God look like?"*
Abraham	*"I don't know, I couldn't see him"*
Sarah	*"Well, where does he want us to go?"*
Abraham	*"He said he would tell us when we got there, and by the way I think we are supposed to take my nephew Lot with us."*

I am not sure about you, but I do not know if my conversation with Michelle would go so well if I came to her with a similar situation. Abraham and Sarah would have to live in tents, be strangers in foreign lands and alter their lifestyles in such a way that their marriage relationship would constantly be challenged as a result of pursuing God's promise. Why did they choose to obey? What compelled them to take such a huge risk and leave all that was comfortable behind? The writer of Hebrews gives us the answer to these questions: ***"Because they were seeing into a future where they would someday live in a heavenly city designed and built by God." (Hebrews 11:10)*** When Abraham made the decision to go he was seeing his family's future through the eyes of eternity. It is imperative for us to make decisions about our children's life with an eternal outlook. Stop looking at the problems and seeing failure. I heard a preacher say one time, "Your outlook determines your outcome." The great leaders of history looked into the future and saw something great. John F. Kennedy saw a future where, "We will put a man on the moon by the end of this decade." Martin Luther King saw a future where, "Men and women would not be judged by the color of their skin, but by the content of their character." And Ronald Reagan saw a time where Mr. Gorbachev would, "Tear down this wall." We need to look into our children's future and see the same kind of greatness. God wants to give each of us an eternal vision over the lives of our children.

I have vivid memories of my childhood home in East Texas. I spent the first nine years of my life living next door to my Pentecostal preaching grandparents. There were some major drawbacks to being so close to my dad's parents. They owned no television so being entertained by Hollywood while at their house was not an option. The thundering fire and brimstone messages from Grandpa still resonate in my ears *("television is Satan's tool" was one of his favorites)*. Also, after every meal with my grandparents *(being a young family with not much money, my parents ate with them as much as possible)*, everyone would go into the living room to read a chapter in the

Bible and then get on their knees to pray *(most of my intercession was spent counting to 1000, because what eight year old boy can pray for what at the time seemed like forever)*. I am still emotionally scarred by having to perform my first and only vocal solo *(Little Stevie's "I Saw the Light")* for a Sunday morning audience. Then there is the time when my grandfather noticed me talking during one of his Sunday night messages and proceeded to invite me up on the platform to sit behind him during the remainder of the service.

I would seem to have been the perfect candidate to turn my back on my spiritual heritage and rebel against all the religious rules that were forced upon me as a child. It might surprise you, but I do not see the aforementioned stories in a negative light. I remember these and other events in my life as spiritual deposits in a yet unformed faith. If I close my eyes I can still smell the intoxicating aroma of Grandma Ferguson's fried chicken and dumplings. I can recall the unconditional love and acceptance I felt when I barged into their house unannounced. But most of all, I can remember these words from my grandfather every time we talked about spiritual things, "Tim, someday, you're going to be my little preacher." My response at the time, "No Grandpa, I'm not, I want to be a basketball player." I was only a boy and all I could see was a future where I would be like John Havlicek or Jerry West. Where I saw fame and fortune, he saw eternity. He saw a future over my life where I would serve God in a local church and in the pulpit like him. He saw a future where I would spend my life helping others discover the life changing message of the gospel. My grandfather died when I was eighteen but his vision would shape the course of my life. Whenever I would struggle with my faith as a young adult I would remember the eternal outlook my grandfather had seen for me. His seeing me as his "little preacher" would keep me on a path for a hope and a future. Seeing your children in the ministry is not the point. What is important is that you hear from God regarding what you see for their future. Too many parents or guardians see a future over their children with the world's wisdom and not with spiritual eyes. Make sure what you see for your children has eternal value.

WHAT YOU SEE SHOULD SEEM IMPOSSIBLE

The story of David and Goliath is quite possibly the most well-known miracle in the Old Testament. When it comes to seeing the impossible no one really compares to the life of David. His ability to see the best when facing unbelievable odds is quite remarkable when you study the circumstances surrounding his life. As the youngest of eight sons he was assigned the thankless task of taking care of his father's sheep. He was so overlooked by his family that he was not invited to the feast when the great prophet Samuel came to the house of Jesse planning to anoint one of his sons as the next king of Israel. To make matters worse, when the war with the Philistines broke out, he was not allowed to enlist in the Israeli army. David's father embarrassed his son even further in 1 Samuel 17 by sending David to the battlefield in order to bring bread and cheese to his three older brothers who were fighting in Saul's army. David had already killed a lion and a bear with his bare hands, and I am sure at night he had dreams of heroic military exploits. But his job, on this day, was to bring lunch to his more important brothers.

Take a moment and put yourself in David's place as he first steps foot on the hill with the Israeli army overlooking the Valley of Elah. He arrives at camp at the precise moment that the armies are forming their battle lines. Two things immediately stand out to him. First, he sees the Philistine champion, Goliath. This warrior stood over nine feet tall clothed in armor that weighed more 125 pounds and carried a fearsome spear designed to impart the most possible damage to a human body. Goliath then steps out and challenges any of the soldiers of Israel to a one-on-one death match. The second thing David notices is the response of Saul's army. As soon as they saw the giant they all ran from him petrified with fear. Does this sound familiar? The entire army had no giant killers. They only saw Goliath through their "grasshopper eyes." David however, looked beyond Goliath's massive size, strength and military experience. David did not see the possibility of failure or death at the hands of a powerful enemy. No, he saw something else. He saw an enemy defying the armies of the living God. He saw an opportunity to receive a reward from the king for killing the "uncircumcised Philistine." When confronted with an impossible situation David saw victory while everyone else was seeing defeat.

I love David's confidence. Every other soldier had run away in fear when Goliath challenged them every morning. Not David. He had the swagger to go to Saul with his boast, he had the bravery to step on the battlefield to confront a giant and he had the courage to run toward Goliath after he had threatened to feed David's body to the birds and animals of the field. What made him so confident? Goliath may have had a big sword and shield, but David had the Lord. He knew that the same God who had helped him defeat wild animals when he was just a young shepherd was available to help him defeat the massive opponent who stood before him.

Do not be overprotective when your son or daughter has some impossible dream. The same God who was with David when he faced the Goliath is still alive to help our children face their modern day giants. Resist the urge to be like David's brothers who made fun of his faith and listed all the reasons *(shepherd of a few sheep, wicked and full of pride)* that he would not be able to defeat a giant. Too many times when our children begin to share their dreams with us we begin to tell them why they should choose another path. What we see, what our children see through the eyes of the Spirit might seem impossible, but this could be their opportunity to kill a giant.

Remember how my son David had dreams of being a fine arts champion? When he stood up to fight for his preferred future for the first time, it appeared to me that he had fallen on the field of battle. My first instinct was to protect him from any more pain and gently guide him on a path where he could have success *(playing video games)*. But I learned something from my son during that season of his life. He refused to give up. His eighth grade year he tried his hand at fine arts with the same enthusiasm and dedication as he had the previous year. When district competition arrived I held my breath when the scores were announced at the end of the weekend. To my surprise David would advance *(by the skin of his teeth)* to nationals in photography, human video solo, human video group and short sermon. We headed to a local restaurant with family and friends to celebrate, with unbridled joy, our son conquering the giant of fine arts failure.

Unfortunately for me, I began to look into the future *(Fine Arts Nationals)* and see another problem. *(Parenting victory celebrations are usually short-lived as another giant arises to take Goliath's place.)* What I saw was more failure for my son. I knew that he had not improved too much in his speaking and acting abilities. He was good enough to advance, but I saw no possibility of success for him at the next level. But David was, and remains to this day, a dreamer. He was not satisfied with just advancing to nationals. He was already seeing a national championship trophy with his name on it being placed on the mantle in our living room. He began to practice his solo categories at home in his room with a passion that was remarkable. I would try to lower his expectations of success by telling him he was only fourteen and he would be competing against older, more mature teenagers. It did not matter what logic I brought to the subject. He was convinced he was going to succeed, especially in human video solo *(one person lip synching and creating a Christian drama to a five minute song)*. When nationals arrived in August of that year he performed his human video solo in the first round *(against over 300 other students)* and rushed up to me and asked, "Dad, how'd I do? Do you think I'll make the next round?"

"David you were great, but I don't know if you'll make it because there are a lot of good solos," I replied, even though I knew in my logical mind that he did not have a snowball's chance in Hades of making the second round. "Thanks Dad," he said, as he ran off to the big television screens to wait for his score to come up. I will never forget the moment in the big convention room that day when I saw his name scroll across the screen. "Human Video Solo, David Ferguson, Superior with Invitation." I could not believe it. He had made the second round at nationals. Our previous conversation repeated itself after second round only this time I was even more certain David was not going to make the final round *(the 10 best human video solos in the country)*. He was not good enough. His dream was impossible. Yet my son saw something in his future that was impossible and had a faith that defied my logic. He would make the final round and would finish sixth in the nation that year in Human Video Solo.

The story is not finished there. He continued to see the impossible and work on his fine arts craft with an intensity that amazed me. By the time he graduated high school he had accumulated over $25,000 in fine arts scholarships. He advanced to the final round at nationals in the succeeding years fifteen times *(including six top 5 finishes his senior year)*. He would win a national merit award *(championship)* in digital photography and the 7th grade David, the worst teenage public speaker I had ever heard, would place in the top ten of the nation in short sermon his junior and senior years. Now he is in Bible College studying pastoral ministries with a dream of being an evangelist someday. Like his namesake, King David, when asked the question, "What do you see?" He saw the best. I no longer question David's or Paul's or Susanna's God-given dreams with my fact-driven, logical mind. I see the best. I encourage you to do the same when it comes time to dream over your son's or daughter's future.

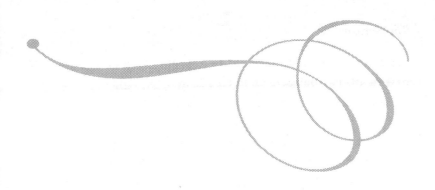

CHAPTER 3

SPEAK THE BEST

"The tongue has the power of life and death, and those who love it will eat its fruit."

Proverbs 18:21

"Your word stands through the ages
Your word shatters the darkness
In you we are more than conquerors
You speak strongholds surrender
Your name overcomes the enemy
In you we are more than conquerors...
You (God) have the last word
It is finished."

Elevation Worship - Last Word

I have always been a sports fan. The hours I spent as a boy playing basketball, baseball and football in the front yard with my dad are some of my best childhood memories. When it came my time to run my own race as a parent it was important to me *(but not always sure it was wise)* that I passed my love for sports on to my children *(succeeded with the boys, but failed with my daughter, except for figure skating)*. Over the years my sons and I have bonded over our mutual interest in major sporting events. Even when normal teenage emotional distance would occur during their high school years, we could always talk sports. So you can understand how much I look forward those special moments every four years when we come together as patriotic Americans to cheer the USA on to victory in the Olympics and World Cup Soccer *(yes I know the rest of the world calls it football, but England coined the term, "soccer" so its ok if we use it instead)*.

One year in early December, I found myself in front of my computer wondering which three countries would be selected as the U.S. Men's team first round opponents in Brazil at the World Cup the following summer. The announcement came. We drew Ghana, Portugal, and Germany. I am not sure how much you know about World Cup Soccer, but only two teams can advance out of the four teams in a country's group to the round of 16. My oldest son, Paul, called me from college and asked, "Dad, did you see the U.S. World Cup draw?" I replied with my usual positive outlook on life. "Yes, I watched it...our World Cup is over before it's even started. We'll never advance out of that group." The three teams the United States would have to play in the first round represented an impossible task for a team still considered by the rest of the soccer world to be not ready for World Cup glory. But I was not the only negative voice about Team USA chances that year. The sports media immediately labeled the US World Cup draw as the "Group of Death."

Why am I telling you a story about World Cup soccer in a parenting book? Because the following spring, sports media giant ESPN began airing a commercial that affected what I believed about our chances at that year's World Cup. A single commercial changed the way I talked about the team.

What was the commercial? Why did it have so much impact? First, there is video of a sea of patriotic fans dressed in red, white and blue, softly chanting, *"USA, USA, USA"*. We see highlights of Team USA's greatest moments of the qualifying rounds as the camera cuts away to an image of a lone fan dressed in a Revolutionary War costume leading a cheer to the roaring crowd. It goes like this...

> *"I...*
> *I believe...*
> *I believe that...*
> *I believe that we...*
> *I believe that we will win..."*

Drums are beating...the crowd is jumping up and down and going crazy...players are making incredible plays. The phrase, "I believe that we will win," is repeated thirteen times just to drive the point home. A tag line, "Every Four Years, The Banner Yet Waves," finished out the one minute and four second commercial.

After watching the commercial for the first time, my American sports spirit was lifted. I began to hope that we could make it out of the "Group of Death." The more times I watched that commercial and others like it over the next few months, the more I believed in Team USA's World Cup chances. They would go on to prove all the experts *(and non-experts like me)* wrong and advance out of the "Group of Death."

What did I learn or relearn from this experience? How can this story help you as a parent with your son or daughter? It's simple. Instead of rehearsing over and over your child's weaknesses and failures with your words, begin to speak of their best actions and character qualities. One of the most important truths to remember when it comes to being a parent is this, your words have power. If you want the best to come it is important to speak the best.

I BELIEVE THAT WE WILL WIN

It's easy to know that we should speak life over our children and not death. But if you are bound by fear or have a tendency to view life like the ten loser spies then it is very difficult to summon words from your mouth that declare a best is yet to come future over your family. James describes our tongue as a ***bit in the mouth of a horse*** and a ***very small rudder that steers a large ship (James 3:3-4).*** He is telling his readers that a small part of your body has the power to direct your life and the lives of those you care about. Finally, he describes the tongue ***as a fire…a restless evil, full of deadly poison (James 3:6-7).*** Nothing will shape the course of the lives of your children like the words that you choose to speak over them. Repeat after me, over and over again, "I believe that my son…I believe that my daughter will win."

The Bible is full of great men and women who were inspired by the words spoken over them. Esther was told by her uncle Mordecai that she had ***come to the royal position for such a time as this (Esther 4:14).*** Gideon was addressed by the angel of The Lord as a "mighty warrior" and when Jesus told Peter to "feed my sheep," it was a word to let Peter know that one day he would show courage and glorify God with his death. These prophetic declarations would often be in direct contrast to what they believed about themselves and the difficult circumstances facing them. But when the best was spoken over them, the trajectory of their lives was changed. I can hear some of you arguing with me right now. You're saying, "I have tried to believe for years that the best was yet to come over the lives of my children, but nothing has changed. I can't speak the best because there's nothing good to talk about." My answer, speak the best anyway.

Every person tasked with the responsibility of parenting a child is challenged with speaking life while being surrounded by death. How would you like to have been Moses' parents? Their son was born in the midst of Pharaoh's infanticide of every Hebrew boy.

When Amram and Jochebed saw that their son was special, they proceeded to disobey the king's law and hide their son from the authorities for three months. His mom would ultimately have to place her precious son in a basket in the Nile River and entrust his future to The Lord. God intervened and Pharaoh's daughter rescued Moses and raised him as her own son. Think about how proud Moses' parents must have felt during those years as their son was *educated in all the wisdom of the Egyptians and was powerful in speech and action (Acts 7:22).* I am sure they felt the loss of Moses around their home, but they were filled with faith that their son might someday be God's answer for their deliverance from bondage.

But when Moses turned forty, everything changed. His anger led to the murder of an Egyptian and he spent the next forty years of his life as a fugitive from justice on the backside of the Midian desert. Did Amram and Jochebed continue to speak the best? I do not know. Their names disappear from Biblical history. It is most likely that they died while Moses was hiding in the desert. His promised future was nothing but an unfulfilled hope. But at the age of eighty, somewhere in the third heaven God began to softly speak life over Moses. I can hear him declaring, "I believe that you (Moses) will win." Moses has no idea when he approaches the burning bush that God's promise to his parents eight decades earlier was about to be fulfilled. The timing seems counterintuitive. Jochabed and Amram are long dead and Moses himself no longer can say anything positive about his life. Listen to his words, "I'm nobody...Pharaoh won't listen to me...I'm a terrible speaker...Please send someone else." His words are full of years of disappointment and failure, yet God speaks the best over his life. "You're going to be my deliverer." Moses finally responds to God's spoken word and walks forward into history.

This is the heartbeat of a faith-filled parent. When it looks bad, speak life. When the facts say your children will never overcome the enemy's attack against their soul, declare victory with your mouth.

What you say matters. Your words are released into the spirit realm and God begins to act on behalf of your sons and daughters.

One of my favorite experiences as a dad was being able to coach my two sons during their high school basketball career. I had started coaching junior high basketball in my early twenties and had moved up at our school to coach high school varsity basketball for thirteen years. The demands of youth ministry led me to step down from coaching when Paul and David were just elementary students. I was a little disappointed, because it had always been a secret dream to watch my sons achieve athletic fame under my brilliant tutelage. But God always knows the desires of our hearts, and after our boys basketball coach left just before Paul's freshman basketball season, I was asked if I would step back into the head coaching position.

This began a journey that would find me on the bench eighteen months later locked in a fierce battle with Lake Country High School in a regional final matchup with a trip to the Final Four on the line. Even though I had coached for years, I had never achieved much playoff success. To this point in my career, I had led my varsity teams to a total of two playoff victories in fifteen years *(one being a week prior to this regional final game)*. This game was special for a number of reasons. First, my son Paul was now a sophomore and I was his head coach for the first time. Second, Michelle was sitting on the bench next to me keeping our book, because there was no room for her at the scorer's table. Finally, Lake Country was 34-1 and heavily favored to destroy us. We jumped out to an early lead and for over three quarters we were ahead by anywhere from twelve to fifteen points. In the middle of the fourth quarter our opponent started playing with desperation and our lead began to slip away. With about two minutes to go, they were only three points behind and I saw my lifetime dream of coaching my son in a Final Four game vanish before my very eyes. I was already feeling the pain of a devastating sports loss. All of sudden I hear Michelle say something next to me *(it's never really a good idea to have your spouse sitting next to you on the bench when you're coaching a big game)*. Her words? "Are we going to lose this game?" Remember, I'm a negative person. I see the dark side of life. I often make the mistake of examining the facts and then proceed to speak accordingly. Lake Country was a better basketball team than us. I knew it. We had played great and they had been overconfident and had played poorly. But now, they were serious about this game and our playoff run was about to end. But in that fourth quarter I had a God-moment. I turned to Michelle and said, "Yes, we're going to win." I believed that we would win and I said it out loud. I spoke the best. Did my words have an impact on the outcome? Does God care about a high school basketball game? I do not have the answers to these questions because I am not that smart. But I do know that in one of the darkest moments of my coaching career, I chose to go against what I thought was true about my team. I spoke life. We advanced to the Final Four and ultimately lost the State Championship game the following weekend. But the next year, Paul's junior year, we held the State Championship trophy above our heads as I celebrated a shared dream with my oldest son. This is the lesson I remember every time I feel like the enemy is trying to defeat a dream over the lives of my sons and daughter. What comes out of my mouth will not be based only on my assessment of all the facts. What comes out of my mouth will be based on my God-given hopes and dreams for their future. "I believe that my children will win." Paul, David and Susanna will serve the Lord faithfully. They will find a Godly spouse and give Michelle and me many grandchildren. They will walk in God's call on their lives and have an occupation that glorifies God. But I have learned something else about my mouth. If I am going to speak the best there is something else I have to deal with first.

DROP YOUR SWORD

Even as I write about the importance of speaking the best, those closest to me *(especially my children)* might have an opinion that I am being a little hypocritical. The next few pages will be the part of this book that I personally struggle with the most. I am definitely not the person that should be given the assignment about the importance of speaking the best. Why not? It's because there is nothing that challenges my walk with The Lord like the words that come out of my mouth.

David's son, Solomon, pens the following saying; ***"Reckless words pierce like a sword, but the tongue of the wise brings healing." (Proverbs 18:12)*** The word reckless comes from the Hebrew word *"batah,"* and means "to babble...to blurt out...to shout angrily." Our modern definition (dictionary.com) of reckless is to "be careless" or to "show no regard for the consequences of your actions." If we allow words to come out of our mouths without a concern of how it will impact our children, then we are causing lasting damage to their spirits. Solomon describes our reckless words as a sword that has the spiritual power "to stab...to jab...to slash...to cut...to slice...to wound and to even kill."

In the immortal words of Westley to Prince Humperdink in the great movie, "The Princess Bride," you need to, "Drop your sword".

Reckless words come so easily for me. It is like the sword of death is glued to my hand. I want to drop my sword, but before I even know what is happening, words of a poisoned fruit are being given to the ones I care about the most. Our words should breathe life, not death. If we want to change our speech patterns, then there are two types of reckless words that we need to consider as we make this decision to drop our swords. Each has a death power of its own.

The first sword we need to drop is the sword of careless words. These are the words that come out of our mouth on impulse or without thinking. These words are often so instinctive that we have no idea the damage we have left behind with our slicing and dicing.

It is words like, "You'll never amount to anything. You're such a loser. What's wrong with you? Can't you do anything right?" This brief list of phrases is only a few of the impulsive words available to our tongue. It's imperative for us to consider James' words in when he instructs us to *be quick to listen and slow to speak (James 1:19)*. As for me, my careless words are much more inclined to be sarcastic instead of being directly negative. I hesitate to give a list of my favorite sarcastic sayings because it might cause you, the reader, to wonder if I am qualified to give parenting advice. But right now, you are most likely thinking of your own list of the careless words that come out of your mouth on a daily basis. Why do we need to drop this sword? It is because these sayings have a powerful, negative impact on the hearer. They do lasting damage and leave visible scars. Hasty, sarcastic, rash words pierce like a dagger. Drop your sword.

The second sword we need to throw down is the sword of anger. As you recall from an earlier chapter I was raised in a Pentecostal home and the biblical principles imparted into my life as boy resulted in a disciplined life that was free of drugs, alcohol or sexual immorality. I could spend some time patting myself on the back, but then God is quick to remind me that throughout my life I have waged a spiritual battle with the angry words that come so effortlessly out of my mouth.

My list of examples of using the sword of anger in parenting is so long that it would take an encyclopedia set of books to chronicle them all. But there is the time when Paul was about ten years old and we were in our van *(all parents with three young children need a van)* traveling back from my parent's home in East Texas. It was lunch time but I was in a hurry to get home so we pulled into the drive through lane at Burger King. Everyone gave their order to me, I relayed it to the fast food employee over the speaker and we headed to the pay window. She gave us our meals and I pulled out onto the interstate while Michelle started handing out the food to the children in the back. It is at this moment in time that Paul decided to test my ability to drop my sword of anger. Somehow Burger King had put mayonnaise *(Paul hated mayonnaise)* on his hamburger and when he took his first bite, he threw his hamburger down on the floor of the van and started angrily *(sins of the father)* yelling at me for getting his order wrong.

When I was growing up, my dad had these great parenting sayings *(more on this in the last chapter)* that reminded us of who was in charge of the family decisions. These all came to my memory as I began to slightly raise my voice *(maybe more than slightly)* and point out to Paul what an ungrateful, unthankful son he was. My anger clouds my memory of all the things I might have said. But the final outcome of the road trip conversation that day was Paul would never have another meal from our hand until he ate the hamburger he threw on the floorboard. As Paul's hunger strike reached almost 36 hours I began to realize my sword of anger might have been a mistake. How was I going to explain to CPS about the importance of parenting discipline versus not providing food for a small child? We finally settled on a compromise where he would have to take a single bite and swallow it. I learned a valuable parenting lesson about how my anger could lead to reckless words that I would later deeply regret.

I would be remiss to leave this subject without touching on the explosive danger that occurs when we combine careless words with anger in the same conversation. If you will recall earlier in this chapter, we took a look at the life of Moses. Moses was a remarkable individual in the Old Testament. His story still speaks to us in the twenty-first century. Movies about his life are scattered throughout our cinematic history. Even as I write this, I'm thinking of the major motion picture about the life of Moses that is about to be released this Christmas. Moses was a prince of Egypt. He delivered the children of Israel by calling down from heaven the ten plagues upon Pharaoh and his people. He carried the stone tablets of the Ten Commandments down Mt. Sinai. He authored the first five books of the Old Testament. He was the man whose final epitaph read, "There has never been anyone like Moses who spoke face to face with God like a friend." Moses was so loved by God that He sent the archangel Michael to fight with Satan over the physical body of Moses after his death. God himself would bury Moses' body. I mean it does not get any better for your heavenly future if you have the creator of the universe planning and executing your funeral.

This is just a partial list of Moses' life accomplishments. Yet, there is a significant moment in his life where he allowed his penchant for anger to be combined with impulsive words that changed the destiny of his life and the children of Israel. The setting of his destructive, reckless words is found in the desert. Moses and the children of Israel are on the precipice of finally entering the Promise Land after forty years of wandering in the wilderness as a result of their lack of faith based on the report of the ten spies. The generation that had witnessed all the miracles of Egypt had died, but the spirit of reckless words lived on in their children. Numbers describes a story about how the new generation of Israel was complaining about their lives in the wilderness. Their grumbling strikes a familiar chord. Forty years have passed and even though their parents have now all died on the journey, they had learned something from their example. They learned how to have a bad attitude and criticize God and their leadership. Listen to their words; *"We should have died with our parents. Why did God bring us out of wonderful Egypt into this terrible place? It has no grain or figs, grapevines or pomegranates. And there is not water to drink!" (Numbers 20:3-5)* The most valuable lesson in this Bible story is the realization that your children will learn how to walk by faith or walk by fear based on the words they have heard come out of your mouths.

God in his infinite mercy instructs Moses to go and speak to a nearby rock and he will provide water. Forty years earlier, God had told Moses in a similar situation with their parents, to strike a rock to produce water. I am sure Moses is having flashbacks of living around spoiled, selfish children for the last forty years and he allows his anger to get the best of him and he utters these fateful words: *"Listen you rebels, must we bring you water out of*

this rock?" (Numbers 20:10) He struck the rock twice and water flowed out from the rock and the children of Israel were saved. In a critical moment of Moses' life he chose to pick up the sword of reckless words. Because he did not drop his sword, he would forever forfeit his right to set foot on the Promise Land. But even more importantly, he would speak destructive words, "you rebels" over the lives of the next generation. If you ever have spent some time in the book of Judges then you can see how quickly his spoken word over their lives would come to pass.

What would have happened if Moses had simply spoken to the rock as God instructed? What would have happened if he had dropped his sword and spoken the best over the lives of the children of Israel? Do not allow your promised future or the future of your sons and daughters to be altered because you choose the tongue of death over life. If you want to speak the best you will have to know how to control those reckless words. If you want to speak the best then there is one more important truth to consider.

BE A FOUNTAIN OF ENCOURAGING WORDS

Another significant challenge I face as a parent is the tendency to make the same mistake over and over again. This was never more evident than Susanna's junior year, when she announced her intentions to try out for the role of Sharpay in her school's spring production of "High School Musical." Susanna never had any interest in playing basketball like Michelle and I did when we were in school. She was always into reading, shopping and anything related to drama. From an early age she was different from our sons. Both Paul and David worked diligently to develop a stage presence and preaching skills, but my daughter was born for the stage and her junior high public speaking abilities amazed everyone who heard her.

So it did not surprise me that she was so passionate about winning the role of Sharpay. I was, however, convinced that she would never land the coveted role of "High School Musical's" female villain. The reason? Her voice was not good enough. This was not a sermon. It was not a dramatic play. It was a musical role. Not just any musical role. It was a role that would require her to have three vocal solo performances. This tension between your child's unrealistic dreams and their ability to achieve a desired goal through hard work and talent is the place where I usually play it safe with my spoken words. Susanna's voice was good, but I did not believe it was good enough for her to be chosen for a lead part. You might recall that I was a little cynical about David's chances in junior high fine arts, but at least for the most part, I kept my negative words and doubts to myself. This time, not so much. I wanted to make sure that she would not be disappointed when she was chosen to be a tree instead. Every time she would inform me that she was going to be Sharpay, I would counsel her to not get her hopes up *(I might have told her more than once that she would not be chosen to be Sharpay)* and to be content with whatever small role that would be chosen for her.

The day came for the cast list to be posted. I dreaded the moment, because I knew I would have the responsibility to put my daughter's broken heart back together. She came into my office that day with a bounce in her step and a huge smile on her face. Instantly, I knew that God had performed a miracle. She looked at me and said, "I'm Sharpay." My stunned response? "That's awesome, Princess. I knew you could do it." I will never forget the words that came out of Susanna's mouth following my congratulations. "Don't lie. You told me I couldn't do it. You're a dream crusher." Do not misunderstand me. She was full of joy and her words to me were not in anger or bitterness. She was just making fun of all the times in the previous months that I had spoken death over her musical dream.

My daughter's statement still haunts me. Do I want to be known as a "dream crusher?" I want to be a fountain of encouraging words. Encouraging words do not always guarantee a desirable outcome.

There are times when you will encourage, when you will speak the best and your son or daughter will still suffer disappointment and defeat. But I would rather have spoken the best and lost than never to have spoken life at all. How many times as a parent have my discouraging, dream-crushing words halted my children's spiritual destiny? I want my words to inspire, to encourage and to breathe life into their hopes and dreams.

An overlooked, underrated New Testament hero is probably one of the best case studies on encouraging words. His name was Joseph. He was a Levite from Cyprus. He first appears on the early church scene in Acts Chapter 4. If Joseph were an American World Cup fan he would be the first to begin chanting, "I believe that we will win." His life was such a testimony to speaking the best over others that the apostles gave him a nickname. Luke writes that they called him, ***Barnabas, which means, son of encouragement (Acts 4:36).*** His new name gives us insight into his personality. He offered help to others in need *(sold a field and brought money to apostles)* and encouraged them to fulfill God's call on their lives.

His encouraging words are best illustrated by his belief in the spiritual future of his cousin, John. The church in Antioch, where the disciples were first called Christians, sends Barnabas and Paul on a missionary journey to the Gentiles. Luke writes that, ***John went with them as their helper (Acts 13:5).*** The word, "helper," carries the meaning in the Greek of being a slave in the galley rowing a Roman ship. John's duty as a missionary was to do all the behind the scenes work, much like a servant or a slave. He did not find this too much to his liking. Ministry was not as glamorous or romantic as he thought it would be. After the first city of ministry he left Paul and Barnabas and went back home.

Paul and Barnabas continued on to a number of new cities preaching the gospel to the Gentiles and after a season of ministry they returned to Antioch to report their ministry successes. After a while they decided to embark on another missionary journey and John wanted to go with them again. Barnabas said yes...Paul said no. Barnabas was forgiving and saw the best in his young cousin. He was probably saying to Paul, "I believe that he can win." Paul was rational, practical and even judgmental *("he deserted us last time" were Paul's words about John)*. But there was a key fact that Paul had forgotten. There was a time in the New Testament church no one believed his story of redemption. **When Paul came to Jerusalem, he tried to join the disciples, but they were all afraid of him, not believing he really was a disciple. But Barnabas took Paul and brought him to the disciples (Acts 9:26-27).**

Encouragers are risk takers. Encouragers are willing to speak the best even when they cannot be sure of what might happen in the future. Paul places John in the "Group of Death." Barnabas encourages, "let's take him with us...he won't desert us this time...I see potential in his life." This moment in early church history was a turning point in Barnabas' life. You see, he was a prophet, a teacher and a visionary leader. He was the one who brought Paul into the leadership circle of the apostles. It was Barnabas, who was called, Zeus, the father of the gods, on their missionary trip to Lystra. In the first half of the book of Acts, the stories are centered on Peter, Paul and Barnabas. But when he chooses to speak encouraging words over the life of John, it results in a relationship split with Paul. Barnabas is now doing ministry work alone, with only John as his helper. It is at this point that Barnabas begins to fade from the New Testament record. We really never hear from Barnabas again, except for a few brief references in Paul's apostolic letters. His encouraging words over John cost him a prominent leadership role in the early church. Encouragement is not just positive words that you speak to people, but the willingness to lay down your dreams and desires on their behalf. It is the heartbeat of being a parent, of being a spiritual father or mother to a young person.

Barnabas may have receded from history, but what about the cousin he rescued from the Group of Death? That young man, John, would become a spiritual son and armor bearer for Paul. In 2 Timothy 4 Paul would actually ask for John's help when he was about to be executed. The young adult deserter, the one whom Barnabas encouraged, would go on to write the first gospel *(Mark)* of the New Testament. When we speak life, when we encourage, we open the door to a myriad of opportunities for our children. Be a fountain of encouraging words.

In 1872, Dr. Higley was approaching fifty years old. His life was really messed up. His first wife, Maria died from a disease. He second wife left him shortly after the birth of his firstborn son and went back to live with her ex-husband. His third wife, Katherine, died, after being injured in a farming accident. He would marry a fourth time and it turned out even more tragic than the first three. His new wife, Mercy Ann McPherson was very violent and abusive. His relationship with her drove him into the arms of alcoholism. He was so afraid of her temper that he had to take his children and hide them with relatives in another state. He finally left Illinois and escaped to Kansas. While living in Kansas after years of family failure he wrote a poem. The poem is called "The Western Home." The words say something like this...

> *"O give me a home where the buffalo roam,*
> *where the deer and the antelope play,*
> *where seldom is heard a discouraging word,*
> *and the skies are not cloudy all day."*

We know this as the song, "Home on the Range." If I were Dr. Higley back then, I would have found it difficult to write a poem full of encouraging words. But even though his life dream seemed impossible, his words were still speaking life. Encouragers are full of hope. They ***call things that are not as though they were (Romans 4:17).*** They speak life to death situations. It does not matter what the situation appears to be in the natural with your children. Be an encourager. Always speak the best.

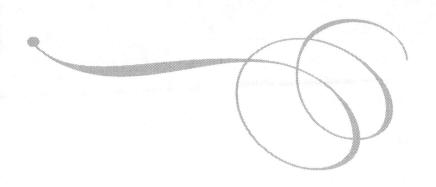

CHAPTER 4

PREPARE FOR THE BEST

"By faith Noah, when warned about things not yet seen, in holy fear built an ark to save his family.
Hebrews 11:7

"The will to win is not nearly as important as the will to prepare to win."
Bob Knight

Tim Ferguson

Due to my Pentecostal upbringing I did not see my first movie in a theater until I was a teenager. I still have 6th grade memories of the local movie marquee advertising, "Snoopy Come Home," and pleading with my mom to allow me to go see it with my friends. Unfortunately for me, my parents were not concerned about their son being able to share cultural experiences with his classmates. They also were unconcerned about how saying no to my desires would affect how I felt about them as parents. We just did not go to the movies. End of discussion.

For some reason still unbeknownst to me, my mom and dad took us *(me and my two sisters)* to see a Disney double feature, "Snowball Express" and "The World's Greatest Athlete," when I was in the eighth grade. This opened an entertainment door in my life that I pursued with a passion. I had always enjoyed reading, so movies were a whole new way to live vicariously through the action and romance portrayed upon the big screen. I loved everything about the movie theater. The previews of upcoming attractions, the intoxicating aroma of buttered popcorn, and the feel of an ice cold drink in your hand as tensions rose during a key dramatic scene. During my teenage and young adult years, I found myself attending every mainstream movie release with either my girlfriend or my movie posse *(Jose, Steve, Rick and Derek)*. You probably could have called me a "movie addict." Popular films like, "Star Wars," "Raiders of the Lost Ark," and "Caddyshack" saw me in attendance so many times that I would lose count of the number of viewings. Most of the movies I saw during this fifteen year period of my life were harmless entertainment as these films were a way to escape from the routine of high school or college life for a couple of hours. A problem developed in my mid-twenties as I began to grow in my relationship with the Lord. The Holy Spirit began to speak to me about the content of some of the movies I was watching and for the first time in my life I began to consider how the language, sex or violence in certain films was affecting some of my life decisions. This was around the time that I started dating Michelle and I quickly

52

discovered that her idea of "going to the movies" was much different than mine. She was not as obsessive and the movies she wanted to see were much more family oriented. The best way to describe her pure heart is to tell you about the time she was seventeen and her friends took her to see her first "R" rated movie, Harrison Ford's "Witness." She came home and confessed her "sin" to her mom and promised to never do something like that again. So you can see that we might not have been living on the same planet when it came to our entertainment choices. Our dating relationship and subsequent engagement reinforced my conviction that I needed to scale back on my movie watching habits.

Our first year of marriage involved a number of life changing situations. Michelle became pregnant with Paul. I responded to a full-time call to ministry and left my athletic director job to help a friend plant a church in Austin, Texas. But we needed income. So I took a job during the summer before Paul's birth as a roofing salesman in Denver, Colorado. There had been a historic hail storm and a couple of contractors in our church had decided to head northwest for a season to make some quick money. Somehow, I wound up like Jonah, running from God's call, but instead of being a passenger on a boat heading to Tarshish, I found myself climbing onto expensive wood roofs in the Rocky Mountains. Being alone, a dozen hours away from Michelle, who by this time was great with child, was a very lonely existence. This was in the days before cell phones, and long distance phone calls were not cheap. How did I replace the void in my heart at the end of each day? I returned to my favorite entertainment activity. I went to my old friend, the movie theater.

I'll never forget the night only a few weeks before Paul was born that I saw Stephen Segal's, "Marked for Death," in Aurora, Colorado. I do not remember all the details of the movie, but suffice it to say that it involved voodoo, murder and other assorted nefarious activities. I was walking to my car in the parking garage when I heard the Holy Spirit speak to me. "What are you doing? Is this the type of stuff that you want to expose to your newborn son? You need to make some changes in what you choose to watch." I was smart enough to know that even though I could hide my actions from my son while he was young, I knew that there would come a day that he would decide to follow in my footsteps. Telling him to "do as I say, not as I do" was not going to cut it as a godly father to my son. It is at this moment that the Lord downloaded a lifetime parenting lesson into my heart. What did he say? It was a word that I will never forget.

BUILD AN ARK

The story of Noah and the Ark is one of the more compelling stories in all of recorded literature. On the one hand, it is a bedtime story we tell our small children, complete with an ark and stuffed animal mobile that we hang above their crib. It is also the tale of God's judgement of man's wickedness, which resulted in the annihilation of all but eight of the earth's inhabitants. Anytime I read about Noah a number of questions arise in my mind. "Did this really happen? How did the Polar and Koala bears get to the ark? Did it flood the entire earth? Where did they get enough food to feed all the animals?" I can always turn to the internet to view the debate over Noah and the Flood being an actual event. But my faith in the story of Noah's Ark and its historical accuracy lies primarily in my belief that *all Scripture is God-breathed (2 Timothy 3:16),* and in the fact that the Noah's Ark narrative is retold by Jesus, Peter and the writer of Hebrews in the New Testament.

Noah's Ark is not just about animals, a flood, or the rainbow we see after a thunderstorm. It is about how these great biblical stories can speak to us in the midst of our situations and circumstances today. Jesus uses Noah in Luke 17 to help us understand the importance of being prepared for his Second Coming. Peter uses the illustration of Noah building the ark in 1 Peter 3 to describe

God's patience regarding judgement on wickedness. But it's the writer of Hebrews who speaks to every parent when he tells us that Noah **built an ark to save his family (Hebrews 11:7).** That's the word I received from the Holy Spirit the night I exited the theater. "Tim, you and Michelle need to build an ark." The first question I asked God after that word, was, "What does build an ark mean?" His reply, "Prepare for the best."

The previous chapters have discussed the importance that faith *(see the best, speaking the best)* plays in our role as parents. Now I want to turn your attention to the subject of preparing your children for the difficult spiritual journey that lies ahead of them. Ben Franklin once said, "By failing to prepare you are preparing to fail." His homespun wisdom tapped into a spiritual principle that is often forgotten as our children leave the infant stage of their development. Many moms and dads find themselves being reactive and not proactive to the parenting problems that are constantly coming their way. In Noah's day, danger and destruction had been spoken over the earth, but God gave this righteous man a plan to save his wife and children. It does not matter what the circumstances around your family look like. It does not matter if your sons and daughters are toddlers, teenagers or have already moved into adulthood. What matters is that you need to begin to develop a spiritual plan from The Lord regarding the lives of your children. James says, *"Faith without action is dead." (James 2:26)* A lack of intentional spiritual preparation for your children is a recipe for failure.

The best way I can illustrate this is to give you a coaching example. I have been involved in coaching teenagers at the high school varsity basketball level for the last thirty years. Even as my responsibilities as a pastor have grown I still take a few months each year to pursue my coaching passion. One particular year I had probably the most talented team I had ever coached. We had two 6'9" big men *(Division I talent)* and guards who could defend and create on offense. All anyone could talk about was about how good we were going to be and that this was our year to win another state championship. Most people failed to realize the difficult challenges that we faced. Several of our key players also played football and as a result, they did not join the team until we had already practiced and played for over a month. Our coaching staff did our best, but we were not playing very well and we lost several close games. Our season reached a tipping point right after Christmas when we lost four times in the last ten seconds of the game. When the outcome was on the line, we were not able to execute the end of game plays successfully. I knew it was my fault. I could have blamed football or the fact that we had several first year players, but the bottom line was the fact that I had not prepared them for the best. I had chosen to not focus on the end of game execution in practice because I had believed our talent would result in us having a lead large enough to overcome our preparation deficiencies. At the beginning of January, I made some coaching adjustments and we began to spend time in practice on these critical game situations. We began to prepare, instead of just hoping for the best. The transformation was amazing. We won every close game the rest of the season, including two game winning buzzer beaters in the two playoff contests leading up to the state championship. Our preparation paid off. We reached our potential as a team and created memories together that will last a lifetime. That's the message I have for every parent reading this chapter. You must prepare for the best. At every stage of your son and daughter's development there are challenges to their physical, emotional and spiritual future. You need to take steps to prepare your children to overcome these obstacles to their spiritual destiny. Like Noah, before us, we need to build an ark to save our family. We need to come up with a Holy Spirit plan and put it into action. Maybe you're asking, "How do I build an ark? What's the first step?" If we examine the story of Noah I think we find a couple of spiritual truths we need to follow if we are going to bring the best out in our children.

FOUNDATION = FAVOR

The opening chapters of the book of Genesis contain wondrous images of God's creation of the world. God spoke light into existence and then created the land that produced plants and trees of all kinds. With each succeeding day, God said, "Let there be," and the earth was immediately populated with fish in the sea, birds in the air and animals to move along the ground. God created man and woman in his image and placed them in the Garden of Eden. There were a few tragic stories along the way *(The Fall of Man, Cain and Abel),* but God's blessing on mankind continued all the way until we begin to read the first few verses of Genesis chapter 6. This is a sobering passage of scripture. God sees that people are filled with great wickedness and the desires of their hearts have resulted in evil thinking all the time. In pain and regret, God makes a decision to eliminate all the birds, the animals and every living person on the face of the earth. He says, **"I am grieved that I have made them." (Genesis 6:7)**

But listen to the next sentence from Moses *(the author of the first five books of the Bible).* **Noah found favor in the eyes of the Lord (Genesis 6:8).** In the midst of God's declaration of destruction, Noah found favor. Why? It's because he was righteous and no fault could be found in him among the people of his time. He is further described as a man who **walked with God (Gen. 6:9).** What is the parenting lesson we learn from Noah's life? It is impossible to build an ark to save your family unless you find favor in the eyes of the Lord. This is why your spiritual parenting plan needs to be intentional. Being blameless and righteous like Noah is found in becoming a disciple of Jesus. In our time *(21ˢᵗ century),* every child needs godly parents, a personal relationship with Jesus Christ and instruction on what it means to walk with God. Too many parents today are neglecting to build a biblical foundation in favor of athletic, educational or family time recreational pursuits *(sorry about the heavy preaching tone here).*

I am so thankful today for my parents. They had a deep faith and their righteous lives found favor with God. This resulted in their commitment to lay a strong foundation for my faith. They made sure that I followed the scriptural mandate to **not forsake the assembling of yourselves together (Hebrews 10:25).** Sunday morning, Sunday night, Wednesday night, weekday revival meetings, if the church doors were open, we were there. Staying home from church was not an option. If we were sick, my mom and dad would take us to church to have someone pray for us to be healed. I still have a vivid memory of being able to skip church for the first time *(I was thirteen years old)* when my youngest sister, Tami, was born on a Sunday morning. If corporate worship and discipleship is casual for your family then you are leaving huge cracks in your child's faith foundation. Sometimes as a parent we have to feed our children spiritual food that is best for their soul, even if they would rather stay home and do something fun.

My evangelist friend, Robert, describes the time as a boy that he told his Nigerian dad he was not going to church on a Sunday morning. His dad's response? "Son, you have two choices. You can get out of bed and go to church or you can stay in bed and I will kill you. Either way, you're going to church. Just decide if you're going to go to worship God or go for your funeral." I know that sounds harsh, but his dad was just using a humorous exaggeration to drive home his point about the importance of worshiping together with other believers.

Moses gives us a more detailed picture of the type of foundation our children need in the book of Deuteronomy. Listen to these parenting tips regarding building a secure foundation. "**The commandments I give you should be...impressed on your children. Talk about them when you sit at home and when you walk along the road, when you lie down and when you get up." (Deut. 6:6-7)** Your children need the Word of God deposited in their lives. They need to develop an understanding of how to pray. Teach them to be generous and to care for the needy. Cultivate a passion for missions and a heart for the lost. Entertainment, sports and school are all important, but none of these can lay the foundation necessary to help your child stand against the storms that are certain to someday come their way. My parents made sure I had the truths of God's Word in my life. This foundation would protect me from really bad decisions even during the seasons of my life when I was struggling with my faith.

A defining moment in my spiritual development occurred in my life during my young adult years. I had just returned back to my college campus after a weekend road trip and when I arrived back at the school all of the other students had already left for the holidays. I quickly realized that I had left my car at home with my parents *(about 45 minutes away)* which potentially resulted in my being stranded on a deserted college campus. Fortunately, there was a girl who came up to me and graciously *(or so I thought)* offered to give me a ride home. When we pulled into my parents' driveway late that night we might have spent some time involved in an old fashioned "make out" session. She then proceeded to present me with an enticing proposition. It seemed that my generous, attractive benefactor was house sitting for some friends who were out of town. Her proposal? Do not spend the evening with my parents. Come back with her to the house and we could spend some more time "talking." You should know that I was still recovering from a broken heart over my high school girlfriend. We had dated for several years and had kept our virginity *(tough battle)* the entire time. But now our relationship had come to an end *(her decision, not mine)* and here I was in the midst of a very tempting decision. I had not yet made the decision in my young adult life that I was going to fully follow the Lord so the decision of whether not to head back to her home would not be based on my spiritual conviction or deep faith. I will never forget the look on her face when I made some excuse about family commitments and got out of the car and headed into my house.

When I walked into my bedroom I could not really understand why I had said no. Maybe it was because I was afraid of getting a girl pregnant or because I was still emotionally scarred from my recent breakup. But the truth behind my decision that evening is that I just knew that pre-marital sex was wrong. It is not like sexual immorality was a subject that my parents or spiritual leaders ever talked to me about. Direct conversation about sex was something that was just not a part of my upbringing. But somehow I knew in my spirit that giving in to my sensual desires would not be in my best long term interests. Somehow without me knowing it, my parents had instilled in me a foundation of purity that gave me the courage to say "no" even when everyone around me was saying "yes." This foundation created a favor that has lasted to this day. A few years later I would meet my incredible wife, Michelle, and on our wedding night we would both experience the beautiful intimacy of sexual intercourse for the first time. Twenty-five years later and counting, our friendship and intimate love continue to grow, not constrained by impurities from our previous relationships.

The foundation you lay in your child's life today will have an enormous impact on the decisions they will make in their future. I know some of you are saying to me right now that you have laid a strong foundation, but your children have still walked away from the Lord or are in the middle of some really bad life choices. Remember Paul's words, ***Therefore, there is no condemnation for those who are in Christ Jesus (Romans 8:1).*** This is not written so you can beat yourself up over your perceived parenting failure, it is written so you can understand the importance of laying a strong spiritual foundation. It is written so you can understand that the biblical principles and foundation you have laid will return to your son's or daughter's heart in moments when you least expect it. Build an ark to save your family. You do this by building a good foundation and by remembering one more important truth.

FOLLOWING INSTRUCTIONS = SAFE PASSAGE

One of the most difficult tasks we face as a parent is hearing and following the Lord's instructions regarding our children. Too many times we allow our own desires, ambitions and cultural wisdom to guide our parenting decisions. Think about the faith decision Noah had to make when he was approached by God to build a big boat. I think I might have launched into a long argument with the Lord concerning the absurdity of his command. But Noah was obviously much different than me. ***Noah did everything just as God commanded him (Genesis 6:22).*** He simply followed instructions. Instructions that told him what type of wood to use, instructions that told him how high, wide and long the ark should be, and instructions about how many of each type of animal should be allowed to enter. There was nothing about building an ark to prepare for a coming flood that would have made any amount of common sense. Can you see Noah trying to explain to his neighbors what he was doing constructing this massive ship in his front yard?

The best outcome for our children's future will be determined on how well we follow God's instructions on the type of ark he wants us to build to save our sons and daughters. It is important for you to understand that I am not telling you to lock your children away from all the possible negative influences that the enemy might send their way. Our children *(like their parents)* are to be the salt of the earth and the light of the world. They are unable to be these things if we try to micromanage every detail of their lives or attempt to keep them in a protective spiritual bubble. Jesus specifically said at the Last Supper that his ***"Prayer was not for us to be taken out of the world but for us to be protected from the evil one." (John 17:15)*** What I am trying to say is that parents prepare the best for their children when they follow the instructions found in the Word of God, when they consider the counsel of Godly leaders and when they respond to the voice of the Holy Spirit.

Throughout our parenting journey, there have been key moments when Michelle and I have responded to the instructions from the Lord regarding the direction we should follow in building our ark. I remember a time when our son Paul developed a passion for a popular children's television show on the local PBS channel. One day I came home from work and spent my lunch hour viewing this particular pre-school program with my three year-old son *(this is another one of the things that no one tells you about while you are dating)*. In the midst of this father-son bonding moment, I heard the Holy Spirit tell me that this was not something my son should be watching. Immediately, I realized that if I followed through with the Lord's instructions, I would be confronted with relational conflict with those I cared about the most. Not only was this Paul's favorite daily activity, but it also gave Michelle a brief respite from chasing a young boy around the house all day. To make matters worse, the television show appeared harmless to me, and every parent I knew with young children thought this educational entertainment was the foundational piece for their child's cultural development. I responded to God's voice by following Gideon's example *(not necessarily saying what Gideon did was the best thing)* and asked for a sign that the decision I was about to make was the right one and not just over-protective parenting.

So for a month I came home from work at lunch and watched television with my son. For thirty days there was nothing I saw or heard in the content of this show that gave me any clue as to why God was speaking so strongly to me about an activity that seemed so trivial. But right as I was about to resume a more normal lunch schedule and pass off the warning as a product of my over-active imagination, my spiritual concerns were unveiled right before my eyes. What was God warning me about? The main character on this particular day had assembled the other cast members and proceeded to conduct a seance with a crystal ball in her bedroom to help them with a problem they were facing. I could not believe it. "A seance on a little kids television show?" My Bible training filled my mind with these words, ***"Those who practice magic arts...will find their place in the fiery lake of burning sulfur." (Revelation 21:8)*** Maybe seances and other types of occult practices do not bother you, but it really bothered me. It is not that I believed allowing Paul to watch a seance on a little kids show would result in a decision that would lead to him practicing witchcraft. It is just that I knew that God's still, small voice was giving me clear directions about Paul watching this television show during this stage of his life. Michelle and I obeyed God's voice and we directed his interests somewhere else *(Focus on the Family's, "Adventures in Odyssey" series)*. Somehow I believe that this obedient act on our part was one small building block for my son's spiritual foundation as an adult today. Over and over again in your child's spiritual journey you will be confronted with God's instructional voice. Following instructions from the Lord is the key to their safe passage through life. Even if it does not make sense or in the moment it looks like a wrong decision, obey the Lord anyway.

We know that Noah's obedience to God's instructions to build an ark saved his family from the coming flood. But you should also consider the actions of the disciples in the book of Mark as they were about to face their own storm. They had just completed a long day of ministry with Jesus as he taught the large crowds from a boat on the shore of the Sea of Galilee. When evening came, he told his disciples to ***"Go over to the other side." (Mark 4:35)*** These fishermen with years of experience sailing on this lake obeyed Jesus and began their journey toward the region of the Gadarenes. Jesus moved to the back of the boat and went to sleep on a cushion. All at once a squall, a violent localized storm *(common on the north end of the Sea of Galilee due to a valley leading from the Mediterranean Sea)*, came up and began to swamp their boat. The disciples, having forgotten that it was Jesus' instructions that led them into this storm, panicked and woke up Jesus, saying, ***"Teacher, don't you care if we drown?"*** What was his response? ***"Why are you so afraid? Do you still have no faith?" (Mark 4:38, 40)***

It is the same two questions he has for every parent today when we are paralyzed with a spirit of fear and when we go to Jesus in prayer asking, "Don't you care if my children perish?" If we are traveling under the protection of his commands there is a supernatural covering over our family members. Do you think the storm was going to kill the disciples while Jesus was sleeping on the boat? He was on a mission. On the other side of the lake, Jesus would confront the Gadarene demons and set a man free who had been bound by the enemy for years. Trust the Lord. He knows what he is doing.

One of the questions you may be asking is how you should build your ark for your family. I could go into all of the specific details God has given us over the years, but each family is different and God has specific instructions regarding your particular circumstances. Some building materials are the same for every family *(teaching children God's Word and worshipping with other believers)* but for the most part you will have to rely on God's voice to guide your family's spiritual journey. If the best is yet to come, then it is our responsibility as parents to prepare them for the best.

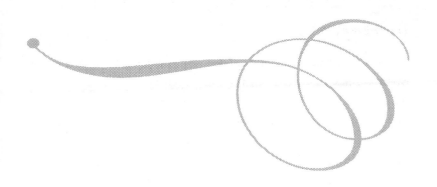

CHAPTER 5

THE BEST DAY

"...Jesus took Peter, James and John with him and led them up a high mountain, where they were all alone. There he was transfigured before them. His clothes became dazzling white, whiter than anyone in the world could bleach them. And there appeared before them Elijah and Moses..."

Mark 9:2-4

"Just me and you doin' what I've always wanted to
I'm the luckiest boy around, this is the best day of my life."
George Strait - The Best Day

"I have an excellent father, his strength is making me stronger..." The words to the song emanating from my car speakers jolted my thoughts from my work responsibilities into the present. My first thought was, "Wow, I didn't know Taylor Swift sang worship songs." Just in case you begin to wonder about my taste in music, it is important for you to know that I was spending the day with my teenage daughter and she had taken control of the song selection from her iPhone playlist. I actually do like Taylor Swift *(so I guess you can question my musical tastes after all)*, but I seldom listen to her music when I am in control of the decision making. Now that the song had my attention I began to listen to the words and what followed can only be described as an embarrassing display of emotion from a fifty-three year old father. I tried to control it, but I could not stop the tears from coming down my face.

One of the foundational principles of parenting that Michelle and I have tried to follow is best defined by the great youth leader, Jeannie Mayo, who said, "He who spends the most time, wins." Josh McDowell, the author, would describe the same principle with different words when he wrote, "Rules without relationships lead to rebellion." That is what I was doing on this particular Thursday afternoon. Spending time with my daughter while strengthening our relationship. Susanna was playing hooky with me *(stop judging)* as we had enjoyed a daddy/daughter date at the mall. A dozen years of parenting teenagers has taught me that sometimes the best way to their heart is through my wallet. So following lunch, a new outfit and a day of one on one conversation, we were heading home.

Susanna grabbed the auxiliary cord, plugged it into her phone and began her random selection of songs. The first song she chose was one that I had never heard before. The words near the end of the song went like this,

I don't know if you knew
So I'm taking the chance to say
I had the best day
With you today

As the tears fell, I turned my head away and thought, "I wish this moment could be frozen in time and treasured forever." Using the words of her favorite musician, my daughter was telling me that our spontaneous day out together was the best day. Somehow in that instant, both of us knew that our current family status quo would not last forever. Someday, far too soon, she will fall in love, get married and begin a family of her own and our relationship will transition into something just as beautiful, but very different.

Do you have a list of best days with your children? Do your children have their own list of best days with you? Young parents are generally very intentional with creating special moments early in their child's life. But as the pressures of parenting grow there is a tendency to allow the busyness of activities, educational schedules or relational conflict to limit the opportunities for best days that are uniquely crafted for each child.

This chapter is inspired by that day in car with my daughter. I want each parent reading the words of this book to experience the joy I felt when I realized what Susanna was trying to tell me. I want you to be able to look back on a lifetime of parenting and not remember the pain, but to remember the best moments, the best days. There is a strategy. If you will put these tips into action then I do believe you will see a marked difference in the relationship with your children.

TRANSFORMATIONAL MOMENTS

There is not a more powerful moment in the Scripture than when Jesus turned to His disciples while they were traveling in the region of Caesarea Philippi and asked them the famous question, ***"Who do people say the Son of Man is?" (Matthew 16:13)*** Their answers of John the Baptist, Elijah, Jeremiah or one of the prophets, tell us that not only did they care about public opinion, but that they probably had done some of their own social research. Peter however, boldly declares, **"You are the Christ, the Son of the living God." (Matthew 16:16)** Jesus responds to this declaration of faith by telling Peter that it was not community gossip, but his Father in heaven that had given him this revelation.

Right now you might be asking, "How does this Bible story relate to being a good parent?" It's because what is described in Matthew chapter 16 begins a narrative that is remembered as a special day by the disciples, especially Peter, James and John.

It is important to understand that this thirty-two mile journey from their hometown of Capernum was an intentional decision by Jesus to have a transformational moment with the twelve men who would be given the responsibility of carrying on his legacy. He creates the atmosphere for this best day by going on a road trip to Caesarea Philippi *(think, our modern Las Vegas)* with his spiritual sons. This city was located in the far northeastern territory of Israel and resided at the base of Mount Hermon, which sat 9,000 feet above sea level. In Roman times, Caesarea Philippi was the worldwide worship center of Pan, a Greek god, who carried the image of being half goat and half human. Most of the worship took place on the massive rock cliff that rose above the city. Followers of Pan had built idols and temples of worship here in honor of their pagan god. This is also the site where crystal clear mountain spring water ran from the opening of a large cave at the bottom of the cliff to form the headwaters of the Jordan River. This particular location was known to the locals as "the Gates of Hades." The people of Caesarea Philippi believed that this crevice in the rock was an opening into Hades so spirits could come and go as they pleased from one world to the next.

Jesus is now well into the third and final year of his earthly ministry. What does Jesus do before he sets his face toward Jerusalem and his ultimate destination of the cross? He takes his disciples to a place that must have surprised them; to the most perverted city in Israel. It is in Caesarea Philippi that he chooses to deliver their graduation address and create a transformational moment.

A moment that would change every perception they had ever had about the Teacher that they had followed for the last three years.

Once Peter opened his mouth and said, *"You are the Christ,"* Jesus immediately responded by praising Peter's spiritual discernment. It was time for a transformational moment. It was time for a spiritual lesson that the disciples would remember for the rest of their lives. Remember, they were looking at the impressive rock cliff displaying all the Pan worship and the opening in the earth to Hades. Jesus told Peter that the car keys of the kingdom of God are now in his hands and all the power of the enemy's gates would never be able to prevail against him. His final words to the disciples on this transformational day, *"Whatever you bind on earth will be bound in heaven and whatever you loose on earth will be loosed in heaven." (Matthew 16:19)*

I think it is this special memory that allowed Peter to overcome his failure of denying Jesus on the night of his crucifixion. Maybe Peter was thinking about Jesus' words at Caesarea Philippi when he looked at the lame beggar at the temple gate, Beautiful and said, *"Silver and gold I do not have, but what I do have I give you. In the name of Jesus Christ of Nazareth, walk." (Acts 3:6)* Yes, Peter would preach with power, heal the sick and raise the dead as a result of being filled with the Spirit on the day of Pentecost, but I think it is also because Jesus had given him a vivid illustration of his spiritual destiny on that day outside the city of Caesarea Philippi.

Six days later, Jesus took Peter, James and John and climbed Mount Hermon *(my commentary on which mountain)* for another best day moment. Jesus' face became like the sun and his clothes turned into a dazzling white color. Moses and Elijah suddenly appeared on the top of the mountain and God spoke to them from heaven. This event is known to us as the Mount of Transfiguration. The word, "transfigured," is also the same Greek word used for "transform" in the New Testament. The Greek word is "metamorphoo." In English, the word is "metamorphosis." Every child in elementary school science know what metamorphosis means. It is the creative process by which a slow, plodding caterpillar transforms into a beautiful butterfly ready to fly into its mature destiny. The Mount of Transfiguration is more than just a description of Jesus glorified body. It is also the transformational moment where the disciples are no longer ugly insects crawling on the ground, but where Jesus is helping them to spin their cocoon in preparation for the coming day *(Pentecost)* when they will be ready to fly.

Every child needs transformational moments. Moments that will prepare them for their promised future. Both of these examples in Matthew 16 and 17 were not accidents. They were specifically designed by Jesus to impart spiritual lessons. What are you doing as a parent to ready your child for a transformational moment? Education, entertainment, or a full social calendar will seldom provide an opportunity for these God-ordained special days. Family outings or athletic success do not guarantee a spiritually transformed life. Transformed moments are found in the altars at the end of a great Kids Camp or Youth Camp worship service. Transformational moments are revealed on missions trips or while your child is involved in helping the poor and the less fortunate. Transformational moments are discovered at the end of a Wednesday night Bible study or during a Sunday morning sermon. They are found when two or three are gathered together in the name of Jesus. The more your child is involved in activities where the presence of God is found, the more likely they are to experience a transformational moment. Do you recall the Jeannie Mayo quote, "He who spends the most time wins"? If the presence of God gets the most time, then your son or daughter will have repeated transformational moments.

A few years ago, Michelle and I went on a trip with our church to Israel for a two week tour of the Holy Land. The emotional and spiritual impact on my life as we walked in the footsteps of our spiritual heroes is impossible to describe. We walked the shores of the Sea of Galilee where Jesus fed the five thousand. I sang "Via Delarosa" on the streets of Jerusalem as we followed the Stations of the Cross. I stood on the Mount of Olives where Jesus will someday return.

When I boarded the plane to return home I knew that my faith would never be the same. The truth of God's Word had become even more evident to my mind and my spirit. I also realized that somehow I had to find a way to bring each of my children to Israel to experience this spiritual foundational moment.

Fast forward two years later. It was spring break, and again I was sitting on a plane heading to Israel. Only this time, I was traveling with my son David in order to celebrate his eighteenth birthday. I was more than a little nervous because I was afraid he would not enjoy a trip with a group of seasoned spiritual warriors from our church who were more than three times his age.

I wanted this trip to be the trip of a lifetime for my son. I wanted him to have a transformational moment that would give him the spiritual courage to withstand the assault on his faith that was certain to come on his journey during his young adult years.

I was pleasantly surprised to find David enjoying himself with the sights and sounds of the trip as well as his willingness to engage relationally with the older adults on our Holy Land team. Throughout the ten day tour I was continually alert for any opportunity to enjoy a transformational spiritual moment with my son. Unfortunately for me, as any parent of an eighteen-year old teenager can understand, David was not so willing to let me inside his thoughts and emotions as we visited each of Israel's landmark locations. The final day of our tour finally arrived and I had yet to observe the moment that I longed for him to have. Do not get me wrong. The trip was a bonding experience for each of us. Something special was happening in our relationship *(we just didn't talk about it to each other)*, but I still wanted an outward sign that God was at work in his life.

Our last morning began with our visit to The Church of St. Peter in Gallicantu. This is an incredible Holy Land historic site. It is a Catholic church that stands just outside the eastern wall of the

Old City of Jerusalem. Biblical scholars say it is quite possibly the site where Jesus was held prisoner at the house of Caiaphas on the night of his crucifixion. It is also believed to be the location where Peter denied Jesus three times while warming himself by the fire in the high priest's courtyard.

The Church of St. Peter in Gallicantu is a modern church filled with beautiful mosaics built on top of an ancient prison dungeon. The culmination of the visit to the church is a descent down a stone spiral staircase into Jesus' supposed prison cell built into the rock. Our tour group of twenty people crowded into the cell as our pastor *(my boss)* gave a powerful message about what Jesus might have been thinking about while being chained in this dungeon awaiting his crucifixion. I will never forget Pastor Hennesy's words that day as his words echoed off the crudely chiseled stone. "What was Jesus thinking about? He was thinking about me. He was thinking about you." We all began to sing *Amazing Grace.* As we started to sing the second verse I looked over at David and I saw him singing loudly with his hands raised and tears flowing down his face. Several thoughts filled my mind. "I didn't know David knew the 2nd verse of Amazing Grace. He does love Jesus, after all. This was the transformational moment that I was longing for."

It was a special moment. It was a moment that allowed me a glimpse into the metamorphosis that was occurring into David's life. When Michelle and I first began to plan for each of our children to visit Israel the financial cost of the trip made us question our decision. We could have used the money for a new car, their college tuition or something more practical. But we believed for a moment that would make an impact on their spiritual destiny. Pursue these transformational moments. You will not be disappointed. Listen to the Holy Spirit. He will guide you on your journey as you search for these best day times with your sons and daughters.

LANDMARK MOMENTS

What is a landmark moment? How does it differ from a transformational moment? Landmark moments differ from transformational moments because they usually occur around specific places and times. According to thefreedictionary.com these events mark an important stage of development or a turning point in history. These are the moments where your child takes a first step, says "Da Da" for the first time or pedals down the street on a bicycle without the help of training wheels. Landmark moments can be your son's first baseball game or your daughter's quinceanera. A landmark moment usually is a sign that your son or daughter is passing from one stage of their development to another.

Even as I write these words, Michelle and I are getting ready to leave for a local Mexican restaurant for Susanna's surprise eighteenth birthday party. All I can think is, "How can she be eighteen already?" The emotions are overwhelming because I know that in a few months she will be leaving for college and no longer be a physical part of our day-to-day lives. Although it feels like I have forever lost the little girl I used to call, "Princess," I understand that this day, this party, is something that we have to celebrate. She has become a beautiful young woman and I reach back into my past to remember that her mom married me when she was only nineteen. I can barely wrap my mind around the idea that within the next couple of years my daughter could be a wife and a mother.

It is important for every parent to be on hand if at all possible to rejoice in these special days. Big games, birthdays, graduations, the first day of kindergarten; all of these are moments that will make spiritual and emotional deposits in the lives of your children as you journey down the parenting road.

The Lord places a huge emphasis on these landmark moments and as a result the Bible is filled with instructions to parents on how to help our children understand the meaning of important historical moments in the Word of God.

For example, the book of Exodus describes the dramatic story of the children of Israel's deliverance from Egyptian bondage. After nine plagues on the people of Egypt, God sets the stage for one last miraculous sign that will finally result in Pharaoh giving them their freedom. In chapter 12 Moses instructs each household to sacrifice a lamb, take its blood and wipe it on the sides and the top of their front door. This blood from an innocent lamb would protect their firstborns from the death angel as he passed by their house later that fateful night. I find it fascinating that God tells them to how cook the lamb *(roasted by fire)*, how to eat it, *(whole lamb, including the head, leg and organs)* and what side dishes to add *(bitter herbs and bread made without yeast)*. He also is very specific about how they are to be dressed *(coat tucked inside the belt, sandals on the feet and staff in hand)* while they are eating this Passover meal. Why does God go into such specific detailed instructions? Could he not have just killed all the Egyptian firstborn sons without having the children of Israel jump through all the Passover hoops?

God created the Passover experience so his people would remember the moment in which he set them free from slavery. Moses proclaimed to the Israelites, ***"This is a day you are to commemorate; for the generations to come you shall celebrate it as a festival to the Lord—a lasting ordinance." (Exodus 12:14)*** The Passover celebration was designed by God so the "generations to come" would be able understand the history behind their freedom. God said that when their children asked about the meaning behind all the weird Passover instructions to tell them, ***"It is the Passover sacrifice to the Lord, who passed over the houses of the Israelites in Egypt and spared our homes when he struck down the Egyptians." (Exodus 12:26)***

Under Old Testament law, every year on the fourteenth day of the first month, the Israelites were to spend seven days celebrating this landmark moment. In the New Testament Jesus changed the Passover celebration into a celebration of the death, burial and resurrection of his body. We call this landmark moment,

Communion or the Lord's Supper. We are instructed to regularly take of the Lord's communion in order to ***proclaim the Lord's death until he comes (1 Corinthians 11:26).*** We need to celebrate these moments like water baptism, communion and significant spiritual experiences with our children. But all landmark moments do not have to be purely spiritual in nature. As I said earlier in this section, there are a number of moments in the spiritual, emotional and physical development of your sons and daughters that need your physical presence during the important events in their lives.

Each step along the parenting road has a myriad of opportunities for marking the important moments in the lives of your children. When our oldest son, Paul, began approaching adolescence it occurred to me that he might need some fatherly instruction about girls *(though I had somehow navigated through my teenage years without much one-on-one conversation about the taboo subject of sex)*. Keep in mind that my family tree is not filled with people who find it easy to share our feelings or to have open discussions about our intimate, private thoughts. So you can imagine my fear at the very idea of talking about this subject with my eleven year old son. This was an important landmark moment and I needed help. So I did what any self-respecting parent does when faced with a difficult situation. I read a book. This particular parenting book gave instructions to give a copy to your child and have him or her, read it at the same time. Then during an appropriate setting we were to discuss the topics written about in the book.

The book was titled, "Preparing for Adolescence," by Dr. James Dobson from Focus on the Family fame. I am unable to remember all of the details today, but what I do recall is that it was filled with themes like puberty, masturbation and other "birds and bees" type instructions. My courageous thoughts went something like this, "There's no way I'm talking about any of this with my son... my dad didn't give me the sex talk and I turned out okay." But he was only a few weeks away from his first day of junior high so I made the decision to go forward with the advice Dr. Dobson had given me in the pages of his book. After all, how difficult could it really be? I was a forty year old seasoned youth pastor with years of giving dating advice and counsel to teenagers. Surely I could impart Godly relationship wisdom to my own son. My son's journey into the teenage years needed a landmark moment. I planned a weekend getaway at a local hotel. We went shopping for new basketball shoes, played video games and watched Toby McGuire and Kirsten Dunst's "Spiderman" movie. Somewhere in the middle of the forty-eight hours, we had a few moments where we talked openly and honestly about God, life, love and marriage. All of the powers of the enemy had tried to keep me from being able to share this special moment with my son. But I broke free from my fear of fatherly intimacy and was able to mark an important stage of development for Paul's life.

These landmarks with your children should be centered, around spiritual or celebration moments. For us, it is buying each of them a new outfit each Easter Sunday to remind them that the resurrection of Jesus is a "big deal." It is the Christmas celebrations with our family, a spiritual week spent at church camp each year or that special day in their lives when they made the decision to follow the Lord's command to be baptized in water. But it is also important to be there to celebrate an academic, athletic or artistic achievement. I may not have been consciously aware of my parents' presence at my landmark moments at the time, but looking back I cannot remember them missing a single important event in my life. Even today, when I have an important moment, I can look up to see my parents who have driven several hours from East Texas to support me.

If you spend the time, you will win the hearts and minds of your children. Invest in their interests, cultivate spiritual landmarks, celebrate their successes; it will pay off in the end.

FUN MOMENTS

"I'm the only guy here" was the thought that kept coming to my mind. Have you ever been on an entertainment excursion with one of your children and wondered why someone has yet to write a book for future parents titled, "The Things Nobody Told Me While I Was Dating"? That is what I found myself thinking as I stood in a line outside a large doll department with Susanna in downtown Chicago.

This particular fun moment idea had started a little over a year earlier when I had purchased a set of books for my first grade daughter designed to inspire a love for reading in her life. My own memories of reading when I was a young boy made me want to be able to create these same opportunities for my children. I can still recall my mom taking me every two weeks to the city library to check out a dozen or so books. Keep in mind that this is an ancient time before Pong, cable television and VCR. Books like, "The Hardy Boys," "Nancy Drew," "Ramona the Pest" and "The Bobbsey Twins" were my doorway into incredible adventures.

So when I discovered a set of historical fiction books, titled, "Samantha," about a young girl who lived in New York in the early 1900's, I knew that this could begin a reading adventure that we would be able share together as father and daughter. But what I did not know at the time was that this particular book collection was a con-game *(I'm only partly kidding)* created by this company to get parents to buy dolls based on the characters in their book series. These were not just any dolls. They were dolls that you could only buy online or at one of two department stores in the entire country. It was not just the difficulty of buying the dolls, but it was the cost. The dolls were almost a hundred dollars each, not to mention the overpriced furniture, pet and clothing accessories that accompanied each doll. Unfortunately for me, being the father of a daughter means that you will inevitably lose many logic-based battles when it comes to extravagant purchases. I said, "No way, we're not paying $100 for a stupid doll." She said, "Daddy please, Samantha looks like me." Her big brown eyes melted my resolve and Samantha became a part of our family that Christmas.

I thought my purchase of the doll would end this "American Girl" nightmare, but I soon learned that there were more books based on different girls in history, which meant more one hundred dollar dolls. Her love of reading *(law of unintended consequences)* led to her obsession of all things American Girl.

This is how I ultimately wound up being surrounded by a sea of daughters and their moms in Chicago outside the three-story American Girl building with my eight year old daughter. Michelle was at ESPN Zone with the boys and I had the duty of brunch *($20 a plate)* at the American Girl Cafe inside the store. No men were in sight, just me. Susanna placed Samantha in her own special seat and we proceeded to eat our breakfast while Samantha enjoyed her imaginary meal and conversation with us. There was nothing overtly spiritual about spending one of my summer vacation days eating with my daughter and her doll, Samantha. It was just a fun moment. It was the best day. Ten years later, I am listening to Taylor Swift's "Best Day" song and writing this paragraph while realizing how much I love my little girl and all the good times we have shared together.

Maybe you are asking the question, "Did Jesus have fun moments with his disciples?" Even though the New Testament appears silent on this issue, I think the answer is a resounding, yes. Consider for a moment how many times it is recorded in Scripture that Jesus went to someone's house for dinner. The religious leaders were primarily upset with Jesus because he was not serious enough. One of their main accusations against him was that he was having too much fun. Their criticism is clearly found in Luke chapter 5 when they asked his disciples why John's disciples fasted, but all Jesus did was party with tax collectors and sinners. Think about how many of the fun moments surrounding our families involve eating. Why do you think that many of our children seemingly come out of the womb asking us to go to McDonald's for a Happy Meal and the opportunity to have fun on an indoor playground? I do not think it is a coincidence that Jesus performed his first miracle at a wedding. He probably was close to the bride and groom and he wanted to make sure that their wedding was a fun event that would be remembered by everyone.

Going back to the Old Testament, we can discover that God told Moses that all newly married couples were not to be sent to war or to be given any work for the first year of their marriage. The husband's assignment was to *stay at home and bring happiness to the wife he has married (Deuteronomy 24:5)*. In the same way, it is important for us to create fun moments for our children.

My mom and dad may not have had a lot of money, but they were experts at fun moments. Summer vacations while camping in Colorado, fishing at our local lake, playing catch for hours in the front yard, going to the library; all activities designed by my parents to do something fun with us. These are the moments I remember. The disagreements and the arguments have long faded from my memory, but the fun moments with my mom and dad only grow stronger with the passage of time.

Do you want to win the hearts and minds of your sons and daughters? Then you should be planning ways to have these best day moments with your children. Time passes quickly. Make sure their best days while they are young are with the Lord and with you.

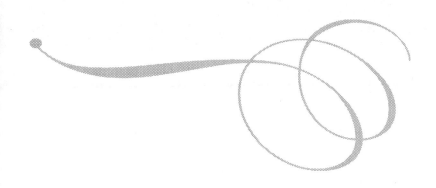

CHAPTER 6

CHANGE IS FOR THE BEST

"When he was twelve years old, they went up to the Feast according to the custom. After the Feast was over, while his parents were returning home, the boy Jesus stayed behind in Jerusalem, but they were unaware of it."
Luke 2:42-43

"It may be hard for an egg to turn into a bird: it would be a jolly sight harder for it to learn to fly while remaining an egg. We are like eggs at present. And you cannot go on indefinitely being just an ordinary, decent egg. We must be hatched or go bad."
C.S. Lewis - Mere Christianity

"For time and the world do not stand still. Change is the law of life. And those who look only to the past or present are certain to miss the future."
John F. Kennedy - Speech in Frankfurt, Germany on June 25, 1963

> *"I, Tim*
> *Take you, Michelle*
> *To be my wedded wife...*
> *For better, for worse*
> *In sickness and in health...*
> *Until death do us part*
> *According to God's holy ordinance,*
> *I pledge you my love."*

On a July Saturday afternoon over a quarter of a century ago, I heard myself saying these words to the love of my life. A few minutes later, our pastor said, "I now pronounce you, husband and wife. You may kiss the bride." There were a number of thoughts going through my mind, but because I was a virgin in my mid-twenties, my focus was primarily on how fast we could escape from the wedding reception to begin our honeymoon. We spent the first two nights in extravagant hotels in Dallas, while waiting to leave on Monday for our all-inclusive trip to Puerto Vallarta, Mexico. It was the perfect forty-eight hours: brunch at the Mansion in Dallas, dinner at the Four Seasons Resort in Las Colinas, watching Robin Williams in "The Dead Poets Society," and as much honeymoon romance as possible. We packed our bags, left the hotel and arrived at the airport ready to check in. It was in this moment that everything changed. For the first time *(and certainly not the last)* in our embryonic marriage, I realized that my life had been forever changed by the declaration of those seemingly innocent wedding vows.

Wedded bliss turned into disaster when the airline was unable to find two seats together for us on the flight. While I was talking with the ticketing agent, Michelle realized that she had her bag with all of her makeup and beauty products stolen as we were standing at the counter. These two setbacks did not initially seem like a big deal to me. I mean, after all, the flight was only a couple of hours long. How difficult could it be to replace her makeup and get a new curling iron? Words cannot adequately describe how mistaken I was on this particular day. Michelle went over to her seat and immediately began to cry. I tried to console her and tell her everything would be okay. But the more I tried to reassure her, the more she cried. Five minutes turned to ten, and ten minutes turned into what seemed like an eternity of tears. I thought she was crying because she had realized that she had made a mistake in marrying me, and now she was stuck with that decision. Suddenly a miracle occurred. Her dad arrived at the airport *(this is before 9/11, so people without tickets could come to the departure gate)* to see us off.

He did not waste time with words. He immediately went on a search and found the person carrying Michelle's stolen bag. When he sat down beside her, she was still crying. My newly acquired father-in-law reached in his back pocket, grabbed his wallet and began putting twenty dollar bills in her hand. The more money he gave her, the less she cried *(I was thinking, "Keep crying", honey)*. Another couple recognized our emotional trauma, and offered to change seats with us so we could sit together. A few minutes later, as our plane lifted off the ground on our way to our resort destination, I heard the Holy Spirit whisper softly to me, "Change is on the way."

Why am I telling you a story about our honeymoon drama? It is because I like to refer to getting married as the "first death." Please do not get offended by my calling marriage a death. Marriage is a covenant, which by definition, is an agreement between two people to do or not do something. A covenant basically means that something has to die. In marriage, both the husband and wife have die to some of their habits, dreams and desires, in order for the two to become one. This principle of "dying to yourself" is why the bride and groom each blows out their individual candle after the lighting of the unity candle. In simple terms, when you get married, the way of life you knew as a single adult is gone forever, never to return. This death, this covenant, is how God intended it to be. The "first death" is not bad. It is just a big change, but a change that is for the best. Because of the "first death," I have a brilliant, funny, gorgeous best friend to share my life and my bed until "death does us part."

If marriage is the "first death," then children are the "second death." A child being born into your home means that the way of life you knew as a married couple is gone forever, never to return. Diapers, sleepless nights and constant feedings, have a way of jolting change into the routines that were previously established in your relationship. Children bring change, but it is a change for the best. Children are God's way of imparting his legacy into each generation. But when children come into your life, their growth into maturity and physical stature will bring a change that parents are not always prepared for.

The best historical example to understand the importance of being able to parent children through important stages of their life is Jesus. You may be asking, "How can Jesus be a good parenting role model?" After all, he was single, and had no children for the thirty-three years he spent on this earth. Jesus may not have had physical children, but he did have twelve disciples. Most of their three years together involved being famous celebrities due to his teaching and miracle ministry. But as the time drew near for the *"Son of Man to be delivered into the hands of men" (Matthew 17:22),* he knew that he had to prepare them for the change that was to come.

The problem for many parents today is not only do they not prepare their children for major life changes; they themselves are either caught unaware of the change or they stand in opposition to any shift in the status quo. Not Jesus. He not only understood the transformation his disciples needed; he also took intentional steps to provide the instruction necessary to help them navigate the change that was to come.

Strangely enough, the best place to find parenting help to deal with this subject is found in the last half of the book of John. Chapter 12 begins the story of Jesus' last week on earth. He and the disciples traveled to Jerusalem for the Passover and decided to stay in Bethany at the home of Mary, Martha and the newly-resurrected Lazarus. At dinner, Jesus' body was unknowingly prepared for burial by Mary when she poured a pint of very expensive perfume *(300* *denari would be worth $30,000 today)* on his feet. The next day, all the people went crazy with palm branches when Jesus rode a donkey down the Mount of Olives on his way into Jerusalem. A couple of days later on a Thursday evening, he gathered with his disciples in an upper room to celebrate Passover. This Passover meal is where Jesus began to describe the change that was coming for the men who he would now call "friends."

These five chapters in the book of John, starting with chapter 13, are some of the best parenting advice I can give you regarding change. There are four important principles Jesus gave us in this passage of Scripture that will help guide you through the major life changes that you and your children will face in your future.

The first thing you should do is "teach them." What did Jesus do? He washed the smelly, dirty feet of his disciples to illustrate how their future would not involve conquering the Romans, but living as servants to a broken world. He began to teach them about the major change that was about to happen to the Mosaic legal code. Under the old covenant *(Old Testament),* an innocent animal had to die daily for the sins of the people. Jesus took the cup, picked up the bread and used them as an illustration of a new covenant, a new change, where one man once-and-for-all would pay the ultimate sacrifice for our sins. Are you teaching your children about the changes that are to come? There are so many of these changes through the years. There is the moment when you send your child off to school for the first time. There is an adjustment from childhood to adolescence, and the change from parental protection to adult responsibility. Are you preparing them for the road that lies ahead? Even more importantly, are you preparing yourself for the emotional trauma that comes with life change?

The second thing Jesus did concerning change is that he "told them the truth." This is an area where many parents fail to provide leadership for their sons and daughters. We feel that if we keep the uncomfortable conversations from our children then we are protecting them. On this "Last Supper" night, before everything changed in their lives, Jesus told them some hard truths. He told them that one of the twelve was going to betray him. He told them that he was about to leave them and they would not be allowed to follow. He looked at Peter, and said, *"I tell you the truth, before the rooster crows, you will disown me three times." (John 13:38).* He held nothing back. His words of truth prepared them for the coming sea of change. His words gave them comfort during the dark hours of fear and uncertainty, following his crucifixion, resurrection and ascension to the right hand of the Father.

Not long ago, a young man approached me and asked for permission to start dating my daughter, Susanna. Somehow, we had made it through all of her junior high and high school years without a relationship, but now here it was. Talk about life change. I would love to have said, "No way in Hades is any boy spending time romancing my baby girl." But she was eighteen and only a few months away from leaving for college. What was I supposed to do? I heard the Holy Spirit telling me a painful truth. "Change is on the way. It's time to let her spread her wings and fly on her own."

So we decided to let her fly with limits. Michelle and I sat down with Susanna and told her the truth about what lay ahead of her in any potential relationship. I explained to her that the dating process ended one of three ways; you break up with him, he breaks up with you or you will get married. Her reply, "Dad, there are three words you are never allowed to say again: marriage, love or sex." She did not want to talk about the potential heartbreak of dating, but we told her anyway. Change in her life was already occurring and she needed the facts. Do not be afraid to speak the truth to your children as they encounter new horizons on their life journey.

There was a third spiritual principle that Jesus imparted to his spiritual sons that night. He knew as soon as they left the Passover meal, the enemy would be waiting in the Garden of Gethsemane. In the midst of an earthquake of life change, his disciples needed two things: "hope and help." He said to them, *"Do not let your hearts be troubled. Trust in God; trust also in me. In my Father's house are many mansions...I am going there to prepare a place for you...I will come back and take you to be with me." (John 14:1-2)* Jesus is the author of hope. He told them not to be full of despair when the change comes, because he would be in heaven building a beautiful mansion for each of them. Your children always need a hope escape hatch. They need to know that there is someone in their life who always has a place for them no matter how challenging circumstances become. But let me give you a little bit of advice regarding this subject. No one suffers despair during these seasons of change more than the parent. I will often hear Michelle tell the story to other young parents about how she almost hated Paul during his teenage years. Their relationship teetered daily on the edge of disaster as both of them struggled with the balance between his need for independence and her protective maternal instincts. He resisted all motherly love efforts and often spoke to her with a rebellious, sarcastic tone. No matter what discipline we chose he would quickly return to his typical teenage boy behavior. The change was almost more than she could bear. But one day, around the time he was getting ready to leave for college, he sat beside her on the couch and laid his head on her shoulder just like he had done as a little boy. Her hard heart melted, and love flowed freely again. It does not matter how dangerous the storm appears to be during these changes, help is on the way. Have hope that this season of their lives will not last forever. There is a light that is getting ready to shine in the darkness.

Jesus does not just offer his disciples hope. He knows they will need help to adjust to the change. The help that Jesus promises is the Holy Spirit. *"But the Counselor, the Holy Spirit, whom the Father will send in my name, will teach you all things and will remind you of everything I have said to you." (John 14:26)* Your children not only require Holy Spirit assistance, but they will also need help from you many times in their lives during these uncertain seasons of change. I do not know if Michelle and I could have survived parenting without the help of each of our parents *(never underestimate the power of good in-laws).* So many times they threw us emotional, physical and financial lifelines to help us with the difficult task of raising children. Be there to be a helper for your children at every stage of their lives, even into adulthood. It is critical that you constantly rely on the help of the Holy Spirit in your parenting decisions. Sometimes, I think the Holy Spirit was sent by God primarily to provide support for desperate parents. If the Counselor is not on your spiritual speed dial, then you are in trouble.

Finally, Jesus turns his attention to the fourth and final parenting principle. It is the most important thing you can do in order to make it through these transitions of their lives. It is prayer. At the close of the Passover meal Jesus prays this prayer over them, ***"Holy Father, protect them by the power of your name." (John 17:11)*** These changes you are facing, or are going to face, are for the best. But they are not easy, and they are a seismic shift from the way things used to be. When these changes come, all you can sometimes do is pray *(I'm praying a lot more now that Susanna is dating)*. If you are not praying over your sons and daughters during these seasonal changes, then you are not using one of the most powerful weapons in your parenting arsenal.

By now you may be asking, "What are the specific life changes that will occur during my God-ordained parenting assignments?" There are a number of significant changes that happen while your children are in your home, but I am only going to talk about the three major life and emotional changes that every parent has to endure.

INNOCENCE LOST

The joy of birth is an intoxicating experience. The nine to ten month journey of pregnancy culminates in a moment where indescribable pain turns into unbridled joy. There is nothing on this earth like the moment when the doctor takes the newborn miracle from the womb and places a son or a daughter into your arms for the first time. All the feelings inside of you are warm, fuzzy and full of unlimited hope for their future. Everything is right with the world on that first day, and a parent can only see a portrait of innocent beauty when they look at their creative gift from God.

For the first few months of their lives there is little to suggest that there is something dark and sinister inside the small body that sleeps so peacefully in the crib. Yes, there is the challenge of having to get up in the middle of the night to feed, change a diaper or rock a crying baby. But mostly your newborn child just sleeps about eighteen hours a day. They do not move with a purpose or make intelligent sounds. In these moments, you could never imagine your child doing or saying anything to you, or to others that would not come straight from heaven. Somewhere, deep in the far corners of the recesses of your mind, you realize that children eventually become independent and strong-willed. But you are quite convinced that your parenting strategies will succeed where all others before you have failed.

Can I burst your bubble now? Your child is not sweet, perfect and innocent. Your son or daughter has a sin nature just like every other human that has been born on this earth. Paul writes about this topic in Romans when he says, *"Therefore, just as sin entered the world through one man, and death through sin, and in this way death came to all men, because all sinned." (Romans 5:12)* Every innocent looking infant has a sin nature as a result of Adam's decision in the Garden of Eden. Your precious son or daughter does not have a good heart to do what is right. The weeping prophet said, *"The heart is deceitful above all things and beyond cure. Who can understand it?" (Jeremiah 17:9)*

If you have a newborn under the age of one, it is important to understand that there is coming a day when this sin nature will begin to be revealed by your child's outward actions. Every broken-hearted parent of a wayward teenager, or a rebellious young adult, began their journey with the belief that their child was full of innocence and virtue. The problem with many parents, is that they often ignore, or try to explain away with reasoned excuses, these outward manifestations of their child's sin nature. When the change of innocence lost raises its ugly head, it should not take you by surprise. You should have a plan ready to deal with the natural rebellion against authority your son or daughter will inevitably display.

I first started noticing the innocence lost traits with Paul as he was approaching his first birthday. We would say little things like, "Paul, come give Mommy a hug." He would say in a cute, innocent voice, "No!" The look on his face made us laugh as we watched him pucker his lips with firm determination. But it got worse when we would give him instructions regarding his safety, or the possibility of breaking something expensive in the house. I would tell him not to touch my plate while we were eating dinner. What was his reaction? He took his hand and tried to get it as close to my plate as possible without actually touching it.

Who teaches our kids this stuff? Where do they learn to say, "No"? How do they develop the instinct to push the boundaries of obedience from such a young age? It is a simple truth, though an inconvenient one. **Foolishness is bound in the heart of a child (Proverbs 22:15).** Sin is woven into the heart of our children. Their natural instincts will be to speak and behave in a way that will often shock you. This is why there is a stage in a child's development described by many in our culture as the "terrible twos." Trust me, I am not speaking negatively over your child. I am only using this common usage phrase to illustrate the initial battle every parent faces in the innocence lost stage of life. This is an important time for every parent. This is a moment where your son or daughter will seek to assert their will over you, the parent. This is a battle you cannot afford to lose. If their will continually prevails over yours during the toddler years then there is little chance of success during their tumultuous teenage years.

I can remember a defining struggle with each of my children somewhere around their second birthdays. My clearest memory of innocence lost was my first parenting showdown with my oldest son. It all started innocently enough with our weekly family grocery run to our local Walmart *(this is before the intellectual elites decided shopping at Walmart was the unpardonable sin)*. After our food purchases, we were heading to the checkout counter with Paul sitting in the seat provided for toddlers at the front of the grocery cart. We passed by a big display selling Mickey Mouse fishing rods for little children. Michelle offered up a suggestion that I should buy one of these rod and reels and teach Paul how to fish. Instantly, the childhood memories of my dad and Papaw *(my mom's dad)* taking me on fishing trips with them filled my soul with happy thoughts. So, even though we were on a very limited budget, we splurged and bought the fishing pole.

On the way home, I was dreaming of all the father and son bonding moments that awaited our future fishing excursions. Suddenly, it occurred to me that I needed to continue teaching my son the principle of being thankful. After all, there is nothing worse than children who are not grateful for all of their many blessings. I turned to him in his car seat and said, "Paul, tell your mother thank you for buying you a fishing pole." I heard nothing but crickets in the backseat. Thinking maybe he had fallen asleep, or was not paying attention, I said it a little louder. "Paul, you need to say thank you to your mom for buying you a fishing pole." There was nothing but silence. By this time we were pulling into the driveway of our house. I turned around and saw that he was wide awake, but that he had a determined look on his face. I said it again, only this time with a fatherly emphasis channeled from my own dad's authoritative tone. "Paul, tell your mother thanks for the new fishing pole!" He shook his head from side to side with emphasis and firmly said, "No!" For the first time, his cute and innocent "no" was not so endearing. Innocence was lost and the battle of wills was on.

I will spare you the details of the parenting struggle that occurred for the next six hours. Just suffice it say. That I was at war internally with two verses of Scripture: **In your anger do not sin (Ephesians 4:26)** versus **Spare the rod and spoil the child (Proverbs 13:24).**

Finally, late after the midnight hour, his trembling little voice filled with tears, said, "Thank you, Mommy for buying me the fishing pole." By this time Michelle certainly did not care if Paul ever said thank you. The struggle was almost more than she could bear. As I hugged my young son that evening and reaffirmed my love for him, I found myself asking "What have I gotten myself into?" Sometimes during his teenage years, when that same strong will would arise in his spirit, I would go out to the shed, look at that fishing pole, and remember that somewhere deep inside his soul is that same little boy just waiting to say, "thank you," even though all the forces of his sin nature were attempting to take him in another direction. We may have lost his innocence that night, but we gained a glimpse of the spiritual, physical and emotional warfare necessary to lead our children into their God-ordained future.

One last thing, before I move on to the next stage. This is not necessarily a book about how to correct the rebellious behavior of your children. What we did that evening might not be the same things you will need to do or say when you are confronted with an innocence lost moment. There are many different ways to discipline and correct the sin nature behavior of your children. Be led by the Holy Spirit and be filled with love. God will show you the way.

PARENTS IN THE TWILIGHT ZONE

Have you ever wondered what it was like to be the parent of Jesus? Was Mary thinking about the immaculate conception and her son's promised future as she navigated the same parenting road that each of us are on today? How exactly do you raise the child who spoke the world into existence?

Very little is known about the life of Joseph, Mary and Jesus between the Christmas story and the beginning of Jesus' earthly ministry. We know, according to Matthew and Luke that Jesus was born in Bethlehem and the family fled to Egypt to escape Herod's wrath while he was still a small child. After a time they would return to their hometown of Nazareth in Galilee, where the Bible says, ***"The child grew and became strong; he was filled with wisdom, and the grace of God was upon him." (Luke 2:40)*** Other than a couple of references about his circumcision and prayer of dedication, we have almost no information on the parenting skills of Joseph and Mary. I do not know about you, but as a parent of three children, I think it would have been helpful if the Holy Spirit *(Hey God, I need help down here)* had inspired the gospel writers to provide more information on the life of Jesus as a child, and maybe just a few pointers on how they managed his teenage years.

The one story in all of the New Testament that gives us a glimpse into Jesus' life as a child is found in the book of Luke. A number of Biblical scholars think Luke used Mary, the mother of Jesus, as source material to write a portion of his gospel. If Mary is only going to provide us with one parenting example from her son's childhood, then I am going to pay close attention.

I find it fascinating that Mary chooses a memory that spotlights the second major change that every parent will have to someday face. I like to call this stage, Parents in the Twilight Zone. What would compel me to give this stage this particular title? Because in an instant, in the blink of an eye, after years of established family traditions and relationships, everything changes. The problem with this change is that it occurs most often without the parent even realizing it. Seemingly overnight, everything changes. When this change happens you will be lost *(emotionally)* for a season. That is why I call it the Twilight Zone.

What's that you say? You do not believe me? Look at Mary's story found at the end of Luke chapter 2. Joseph and Mary traveled the seventy miles *(probably more, because they would have avoided Samaria)* from Nazareth to Jerusalem at the beginning of each year to celebrate the Passover Festival for seven days. The Law of Moses said the Passover must be celebrated ***at the place God will choose*** *as a dwelling for his Name (Deuteronomy 16:6)*. This annual trip obviously morphed into more than just a religious activity. Like Christmas today, the roundtrip to Jerusalem was a celebration of their faith in God deliverance and a time to spend with family and friends. Every year for twelve years, they took Jesus up to the capital city for the Passover. I am certain that this particular year, everything appeared to be just like all of their previous trips. But unbeknownst to them something significant was happening that would shatter their previous Passover routines. Their son was changing into a man. The Passover Festival in Jerusalem ended and they packed up their belongings and headed home. Hours later when Joseph and Mary stopped for the night their twelve-year old son was nowhere to be found. They probably thought that during the day's journey Jesus was hanging out with his cousins or friends. But after a futile frantic search among the relatives they headed back to Jerusalem to find their missing son. Do you think you have had some rough parenting storms? How would you like to have lost God's son, the savior of the world?

They finally found him after three days *(can you imagine the fear they felt for those 72 hours?)* in the temple courts, listening and asking questions of the teachers of the law. Mary rushed up to him and read Jesus the riot act. "***Son, why have you treated us like this? Your father and I have been anxiously searching for you" (Luke 2:48).*** Jesus looked at his mom and says, ***"Why were you searching for me? Didn't you know I had to be in my Father's house?" (vs. 49)*** What was their reply? ***They did not understand what he was saying to them (vs. 50).*** His statement that he was doing kingdom business had no place in their limited parental minds. What had happened? The son they had known for the first twelve years of his life was gone, never to return. They had entered the parenting Twilight Zone. Jesus was about to become a teenager and everything had changed. Joseph and Mary would be forced to confront a whole new set of parenting challenges as their son prepared himself for God's ultimate plan for his life.

This life transition is unlike any of the other changes, because you have spent over ten years being the hero to your child. Now you will find yourself as a spectator to many of their activities and not a participant with them. If you are unable to adapt to this new paradigm shift then your son or daughter will react strongly *(and not in a good way)* to your attempts to keep things the same forever. If you have young children, begin preparing yourself emotionally for the time when Mom and Dad will not be the coolest people on the earth. Start considering the possibility that God may have plans for your son or daughter that you may have not considered. But the worst part of this stage is the moment that you realize that your beloved children would much rather spend time with their friends than with you, the parent who has taken care of them from birth, loved them and given them beaucoup dollars *(or as my dad used to say, "bookoos" of money)*.

I feel like I handled this transitional stage fairly well with the boys as they entered adolescence. However I was unprepared for the emotional gut punch life threw my way when my daughter Susanna sent me into this Twilight Zone. The Friday night in the fall when everything changed between us still hurts a little bit even today. Susanna was in the seventh grade and we were going to the stadium to watch our high school's football game. We paid for our tickets, walked through the gate and headed for the stands on our side of the field. After a few moments, I noticed that Susanna was no longer beside me and was walking slowly several feet behind me. I turned back and said, "Susanna, what are you doing? You need to hurry up or we are going to miss the kickoff." The words that followed drove a dagger into my daddy soul. She replied, "Dad, you go ahead. I can't be seen with you."

I pride myself on being able to see the next move on the chess board of life. But my daughter's abrupt change from my "little princess" to an attractive, popular junior high student concerned about her image of being too much of a "daddy's girl" was almost more than I could bear. Why was this moment with Susanna so much more difficult than with the boys? I am not sure I can give an adequate answer. Maybe it is because when each of the boys sent me into the Twilight Zone, I still had another child I could lean upon to still do the "fun stuff." Or it could be that my heart was more vulnerable to her change because she was my only daughter, and everyone knows how a dad feels about his daughter.

Joseph and Mary entered the Twilight Zone the instant Jesus said, *"Why are you searching for me?" (Luke 2:49)* I entered the Twilight Zone the instant Susanna said, "Dad, I can't be seen with you." It did not make it any easier even though I knew that this change was for the best. Trying to hold on to their childhood will ultimately lead to rebellion and resentment. This season of parenting requires a skillful balance between their need to still be nurtured and their desire to be about *"their Father's business" (Luke 2:49).* This stage of development caused me to transition from absolute authority into something more like a coach. I still need to direct, critique and correct, but I also need to know those moments when it is time for me to get out of the way and to let them play on their own. It is not easy when this journey commences, but if you stay the course and are led by the Spirit, then something even more special lies on the other side of the Twilight Zone.

HE/SHE MUST INCREASE, I MUST DECREASE

The life of John the Baptist is one of the best examples of faith-filled living in the entire Bible. Jesus himself, said, *"Among those born of women there is no one greater than John" (Luke 7:28).* He was a powerful prophet and his message turned the hearts of many people back to God. In spite of his strange looks, unusual diet and isolated location, John was the most popular and famous preacher of his day. He would baptize anyone in the Jordan River who wanted to repent of their sins. He attracted so many disciples, including the hated tax collectors that the soldiers, Pharisees and the teachers of the law came out to examine his ministry and see if he was a threat to them. His words even penetrated the halls of King Herod. John had achieved the pinnacle of success in his field. When your nickname becomes your last name, then you know that you are somebody really important.

But one day, his cousin, Jesus, shows up to be baptized. Instantly, everything changes. John tells the crowd that Jesus will take away the sin of the world and that he is the man that they should start following. He makes a statement to the people that I think is one of the more remarkable sentences ever spoken by a man. He says of Jesus, ***"He must become greater, I must become less" (John 3:30).*** Or as the old King James Version says, **"He must increase, I must decrease."**

From this point forward, John's ministry does begin to lose momentum. Ultimately, he will find himself alone and in prison as a result of his uncompromising message to the halls of power *(this might be a lesson for us today about speaking truth regardless of the consequences or opinions of the culture).* It is amazing to me that John could see the change coming in his ministry. He knew that it would affect his influence and popularity, and yet he willingly accepted the change because he understood that it was for the best.

The final major transition change a parent will encounter is so far off in the future for many of you, that I hesitate to even write about it. Those who only have newborns or young children will not be able to comprehend a time when the roles of a parent and a child begin the process of being turned upside down. There will be a transformational moment somewhere down the road in your parenting future where you must decrease and your sons and daughters must increase.

I have watched this play out at my place of employment for the last ten years. My boss, Jim Hennesy, is the senior pastor of our church. It is a powerful ministry and his leadership, along with that of his wife, Becky, has propelled us into an immeasurable kingdom influence in our community and around the world. Around ten years ago, his father, Dr. James Hennesy, retired from his position in Florida and came to our church to oversee ministries of pastoral care and our senior saints. Here is a man who pastored one of the great churches of our denomination in Columbus, Georgia. This is a man who was the President of Southeastern Assemblies of God University in Lakeland, Florida. Now he is submitting to the leadership of his son and accepting a position that seems so far removed from the positions of importance and influence of his younger years. But he is a wise dad. He knows the importance of the parenting principle that his son must increase and he must decrease.

I see the handwriting on the wall for my position as the parent of my children. My son David just recently entered into his first serious relationship with a young woman who just graduated from college. Throughout his life, his mother and I have been able to directly guide him regarding his various friendships and "wanna be" girlfriends. I am watching him go through the highs and lows of young love. I stand by ready to offer counsel and wisdom, while recognizing at the same time that his behavior regarding relationships is very familiar to me *(and I definitely never wanted my father's advice about my love interests)*.

So as this change is occurring I realize that I must decrease. My oldest son, Paul, works for me. But a time is coming when I might be working for him and submitting to his authority. Michelle and I are indebted to both of our parents for their financial support throughout our marriage, but a season of change is rapidly approaching where we might need to increase our support of them as their resources decrease.

Way back at the beginning of the book, I said that I was writing this because it was helping me process emotionally through a major life change. It is because I am at the stage where the change requires me to decrease my authority and influence while Paul, David and Susanna begin to increase their pursuit of their own unfulfilled promises.

This change is for the best. It is the way God designed it. If you try to hold on to power and influence too long, it leads to authoritarian rule and it will tear apart the fiber of the relationships you hold most precious. These changes are from God. They are for your good. Embrace each and every moment.

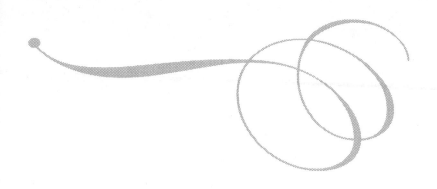

CHAPTER 7

THE ROAD BEST TAKEN

Then Isaiah said to Hezekiah, "Hear the word of the Lord: The time will surely come when everything in your palace, and all that your predecessors have stored up until this day, will be carried off to Babylon. Nothing will be left, says the Lord. And some of your descendants, your own flesh and blood who will be born to you, will be taken away, and they will become eunuchs in the palace of the king of Babylon." "The word of the Lord you have spoken is good," Hezekiah replied. For he thought, "Will there not be peace and security in my lifetime?"
(II Kings 20: 6-19)

I shall be telling this with a sigh
Somewhere ages and ages hence:
Two roads diverged in a wood, and I—
I took the one less traveled by,
And that has made all the difference.
(The Road Not Taken - Robert Frost)

"So you're okay with me giving up my goals and dreams to lead a church of my own and having to be a greeter at Walmart when it comes my time to retire?"

In law school they teach you to never ask a question *(especially to a thirteen-year old)* if you do not know or are unprepared for the answer. Paul's reply, "Yes, I'm okay with that. I just want to keep going to my church and graduate from the school I've attended since I was three years old." To make matters worse, he started sobbing uncontrollably and as I looked up at the entrance to his room, I saw Michelle crying as well. I had been convinced that once my wife and children understood the desires of my heart, they would willingly lay aside some of their relational preferences in order for us to pursue greatness as a family.

At the time of this family crisis, I was forty-three years old. I was making a transition from twenty years of youth ministry to an executive role in our church. In the midst of this change, several opportunities for me to be the lead pastor of a church started coming my way. The challenge of new mountains to climb, new places to explore and new people to lead filled my heart and my mind with excitement. I listened to the offers and began to dream and plan out our family's new adventure together. My family, however, had other ideas. Especially Michelle, and Paul, who was old enough to understand how a move during his junior high years could affect him. But I pursued these opportunities anyway, and now the moment of truth had come. We were getting ready to leave for a weekend to check out the potential new church and city.

Paul's reaction stunned me. I knew he would be upset, but the firm resolve he displayed shook my confidence. Michelle's resistance to any move was something that did not surprise me *(she enjoyed being close to her mom and dad)*, but I was sure her love for me would overcome any doubts she might have. But Paul was a different story. I had worked with teenagers long enough to know how much a geographical move could affect their spiritual growth. My thoughts turned to David, who was about to turn eleven. Was he as opposed to this as Paul? I had not even bothered to discuss it with him.

This family crisis created a major problem for me. We were due to leave for the recruiting trip in a few hours. How was it going to look to a pastoral search committee if my entire family cried the whole weekend? Another big dilemma was the silence from the Lord. I prayed for several weeks about the move, but I had not received any clear direction from him. I had not heard a "no." But there was not a word that said, "Go," either. I went outside in the backyard knowing that I had less than one hundred minutes to make a decision *(Michelle's preference was clear, but she wasn't going to stand in the way of my dream)* that would shape the course of our family's future. I cried out to God. "What should I do? Which road should I take?"

These life decisions are often the turning point in determining the success or failure of our children's future. Parents seldom consider how passionately pursuing their own ambitions and desires can negatively affect the attitude and behavior of their sons and daughters. Be careful when you cry out to God on behalf of your dream. Make certain that those you love are going to be celebrating alongside you when you reach the pinnacle of your climb.

An overlooked parenting debacle in the Bible gives us great insight into the dangers of running down the road of selfish desire without considering how it would affect generational momentum. The story starts innocently enough in the Old Testament when the prophet Isaiah comes to visit an ailing King Hezekiah.

Hezekiah is one of the Mount Rushmore kings of the Old Testament. The writer of II Kings describes him as a man who ***"trusted in the Lord, the God of Israel. There was no one like him among all the kings of Judah, either before him or after him. He held fast to the Lord and did not stop following him." (II Kings18:5-6).*** Hezekiah led Judah during an era that saw the rise of Assyria as a world power, perhaps the greatest empire the world had ever seen up until that point. Assyria had already conquered Israel

(King Solomon's Israel had split into two countries after his death) and had turned their attention to the capture of Judah and the capital city of Jerusalem. Hezekiah's faithful devotion to God resulted in a spiritual revival that ultimately led to the deliverance of Judah from the hand of the enemy *(an angel of the Lord killed 185,000 Assyrian soldiers in one night)*. Hezekiah was also a visionary leader who succeeded in everything he attempted. It is difficult for us in modern times to fully understand the lasting accomplishments of this king. He *had great wealth and honor (II Chronicles 32:27)* and oversaw the economic rebuilding of the infrastructure of a once-great nation. The construction of Hezekiah's water tunnel remains one of the most amazing feats of engineering in history. If you ever travel to Israel, make sure you visit this remarkable archeological find.

I know that this is probably too much historical information for you. But I think it is important for you to know how much power and influence Hezekiah had. He was famous throughout the Middle East because he was the only world leader who had been able to stand against the power of the Assyrian army. But as we soon discover, his successful pursuit of spiritual and national goals came at a cost. His time on earth was over and now the man of God came to visit Hezekiah with a simple message, *"Put your house in order, because you are going to die." (II Kings 20:1)*

At thirty-nine years of age, he was not prepared for the prophet's death sentence. Hezekiah offered up a desperate prayer reminding God of how faithfully he had served him his entire life. He turned in his bed with his face to the wall and *wept bitterly (II Kings 20:3).* Isaiah was in the middle of the palace courtyard when God instructed him to go back and tell the king that he had heard his tearful prayer and that he would add fifteen more years to his life.

God confirmed his promised healing with a sign from heaven that was perhaps the greatest miracle recorded since the creation of the earth. He made the shadow on the steps to the king's palace go backwards ten steps. Now, I am not a scientist, but the only way I see that happening is for God to stop the earth on its axis and make it move backwards ten degrees. You have to be pretty special to God in order for him to change the earth's rotation on your behalf. Hezekiah was healed, resumed his position as a powerful king and finally, at the age of forty-two years old, became a father for the first time.

Up until this time, every major decision of his life had been the right one. When presented with two broad and narrow path choices he had always chosen the best road. He now had the opportunity to pass on his faithful legacy to the next generation with the extra years God so graciously gave him. But Hezekiah made three critical mistakes during the final leg of his life race which unfortunately led to his son, Manasseh, becoming maybe the most wicked, evil king that Israel and Judah had ever seen. Instead of passing a faith-filled legacy down to his son, his decisions during these years led to a teenage son turning his back on the God of his father and pursuing a life of sinful depravity. Studying these three decisions--those moments when Hezekiah chose the worst road--can help twenty-first century parents choose the best road. Our faith and our successes cannot be inherited by our children. We need to discover the best roads and take them as an example to our children. We need to learn how to increase spiritual generational momentum. We do not want our children being labeled, like Hezekiah's son, *doing more evil than the Amorites (II Kings 21:11)* or *shedding so much innocent blood that it filled Jerusalem from end to end (II Kings 21:16).* How can we do this? By choosing the roads that Hezekiah rejected.

HUMILITY > BOASTING

Not long after his miraculous healing, the Bible said *Hezekiah's heart was proud and he did not respond to the kindness shown him; therefore the Lord's wrath was on him and on Judah and Jerusalem (II Chronicles 32:25).* What did he do that upset God so much? He was filled with pride. If your heart is proud then it will affect every area under your influence. His leadership mistake was his inability to resist "showing off" everything of importance in his entire kingdom when Babylonian leaders came to visit him. He showed them all of his wealth, his armory and all of his treasures. Isaiah asked him, ***"What did they see in your palace?"*** Hezekiah replied, ***"There is nothing among my treasures I did not show them (II Kings 20:15).*** If you keep reading in this chapter, then you discover that because he could not resist the urge to boast, it cost his son and future generations their freedom. Walking in humility brings honor, favor and blessing from the Lord. A life filled with pride results in the possibility of our bringing disaster down on the lives of our children. Hezekiah had no idea that proudly displaying everything in his kingdom to a future enemy would affect his newborn son so negatively. I understand that God seems to punish Hezekiah too severely for this seemingly innocent act of being proud of what he had accomplished. But every leader and every parent needs to be careful to resist the temptation to take credit for God's blessings.

Maybe the most dangerous pitfall that awaits young parents is the temptation to want to boast of all the accomplishments of their children. It starts almost from the minute that their son or daughter emerges from the womb. We boast in how much they weigh, the amount of hair on their head or how peacefully they sleep through the night. Do not misunderstand me: I realize how the miracle of birth creates feelings of pleasure and unbridled joy. Our modern language usage of being "filled with pride" is perfectly understandable in the sense that we are overwhelmed with a love that automatically covers over a multitude of imperfections. We are seeing the best almost from the beginning.

But this God-given paternal and maternal love can easily turn into boasting and a ***pride that goes before destruction (Proverbs 16:18).*** Soon we are bragging about how fast our newborn child said his first word or took his first step. The enemy is very skilled at getting parents to go down a slippery slope where the natural enjoyment of accomplishment turns into a heart filled with a desire to show off their children's successes in order to fulfill an emptiness in their own soul. This type of pride is not a good thing. There is a repetitive message about pride throughout the Bible. It goes something like this, ***God opposes the proud, but shows favor to the humble (James 4:6).*** These are the moments the enemy sets up as easy broad road choices that must be resisted. I know from our own personal parenting decision how easily parents can fall into the trap of boasting about their children.

How do I know about this? Because soon after our son Paul was born, we discovered that he was a genius. I realize that you think I am kidding: but at the time, Michelle and I were convinced that she had given birth to the world's most gifted child. Almost from the beginning, Paul was beating all of the world records for baby accomplishments. He started walking at about eight months and when he was about a year old, he was already speaking in complete sentences, with the ability to engage in a back-and-forth conversation with adults. By the time he was eighteen months, he knew his entire alphabet and could already recognize many site words. It was amazing. We were sure of one thing. Either Paul was the smartest child ever born or we were the greatest parents on the face of the earth *(or probably both).*

For a while it only got better from there. He had an amazing memory, so we began filling his mind with an abundance of facts. Before the age of two, he committed dozens of scripture to memory, knew all the presidents in order, memorized all the states and capitals and could name every professional sports team and their mascots. How did we respond to being the parents of a child prodigy? We did what any self-respecting parent would do. We put him on display for all of the world *(or anyone who would pay attention)* to see. Friends would quiz him on these various subjects and his correct answers filled us with a pride beyond compare. I can close my eyes and still see Paul saying, "Oklahoma, the big gun! Their capital is Oklahoma

City." Sometimes I wonder what we would have been like if we had access to a social media network back in those early days.

A textbook example of boasting in the accomplishments of our children is Tiger Woods. He was a golf superstar when he just a toddler. On the internet you can research his television debut *(That's Incredible with Fran Tarkenton)* at the age of five. His dad Earl is seen pontificating on the virtues of the young Tiger. He tells the camera that "Tiger has a concept of strategy. He hits it where he wants to hit it. Not only where, but how." Tiger's dad will only get worse through the years. After Tiger became the first African American to win the Master's in 1997, Earl gave the following quote to Gary Smith in Sports Illustrated Magazine: "Tiger will do more than any other man in history to change the course of humanity...He is the Chosen One. He'll have the power to impact nations. Not people. Nations." Earl Wood went on to compare his young adult son to Ghandi and Buddha. I have always been a fan of Tiger Woods *(I know many of you are upset at me right now, but if I only rooted for faithful believers, then my sports universe would be very limited in scope)*, but for a parent to place such a burden on their young child demonstrates an incredible lack of parenting wisdom. Time and circumstances have demonstrated that when it comes to humanity, Tiger is definitely not the "Chosen One."

Looking back, I now realize the dangers "showing off" can have on our children's future. We told everyone we knew about how Paul's elementary school wanted to jump him ahead two grade levels when he was in the first grade. But we were unprepared for his report card his freshman year in high school when he made a fifty-nine the last nine weeks in Biology. Our genius son turned into a normal high school student who sometimes resisted our efforts for him to walk in academic discipline. He still had the same incredible memory, but we had to accept his weakness and failures with the same love and encouragement *(and the occasional, "you're grounded for life" discipline)* that we did when he displayed his intellectual abilities.

I am doing my best to try and not come off as a perfect parent with perfect children. I know that spiritual danger for their lives awaits around every corner. I can be talking about how wonderful my children are in one moment, only to be confronted with pain and disappointment by their actions the next. Much of the counsel in this book is based on the mistakes Michelle and I have made over the years, or on the response of our children during difficult seasons of their lives.

If you remember nothing else about this part of the book, remember this; do not let your own self-esteem and self-worth be completely wrapped up in the abilities and achievements of your children. Also be willing to accept the positions and purposes to which God has called your sons and daughters. Do not try to live vicariously through them or be disappointed if their life's calling does not meet your expectations. These temptations are the birthplace of a pride that is destructive.

As I leave this topic, consider the words from Jesus regarding our accomplishments. ***"What good is it for someone (your sons and daughters) to gain the whole world, yet lose or forfeit their very self" (Luke 9:25).*** Parents, be humble. Resist the urge to boast. It is a better road. It is the road best taken.

GOD'S WISDOM > COMMON SENSE

Hezekiah's second big mistake was in choosing to be friendly with a very dangerous nation. Babylon's king had sent envoys with ***letters and a gift (II Kings 20:12)*** to visit Hezekiah because they had heard of his illness and the miraculous sign from heaven when God affected the rotation of the earth's axis. Hezekiah would have been on high alert if Assyrian leaders had tried to approach him because their army was an immediate and obvious threat to the safety and security of Judah. The Babylonians, however, were harmless because they were not yet a world military power. Besides, the Babylonians were somewhat allied with Judah against Assyria under the age old proverb, "the enemy of my enemy is my friend." In this critical moment, with the future of his nation and his legacy hanging in the balance, Hezekiah chose to ignore the road of God's wisdom.

A century later, these disarming envoys provided King Nebuchadnezzar with all the historical information necessary to send his army to seize the treasures of Judah. Babylon was never a friend of Hezekiah. They just had to wait a hundred years to have enough military strength to conquer the great city of Jerusalem. The enemy of your soul can be very patient in preparing an attack against all that you hold dear. Only wisdom can protect you. God's wisdom is the ability to think and make decisions based on knowledge, experience and supernatural insight from the Holy Spirit. The New Testament says the ***manifestation of the Spirit is given for the common good. To one there is given through the Spirit, the message of wisdom (I Corinthians 12:8).*** Hezekiah needed to walk in wisdom when approached by leaders of a distant nation. He chose another road. He chose to accept the Babylonian gifts at face value and opened up the doorway to his kingdom without considering the cost to future generations.

Seeking wisdom from above is the best decision you will ever make regarding the future of your sons or daughters. Resist the urge to raise your children based on common sense or what the culture defines as the most important. Just because it looks nice and shiny or because everyone around you is doing something does not mean you necessarily have to imitate them in the same way. Listen for the voice of the Lord. Understand the times. Understand that the enemy has a long range destructive plan against your family. When Jesus sent out the Twelve into the world he told them that he was ***"Sending you out like sheep among wolves. Therefore be as shrewd as snakes and as innocent as doves" (Matthew 10:16).*** Believe the best, but be wise. Or as my dad used to say, "Trust everyone, but cut the cards."

There is no better example for Michelle and I on this subject than the invention and rise in popularity of the cell phone and MP3 players *(small, portable media libraries)*. I will never forget my introduction to the lure of this modern technology. In the early part of the twenty-first century, I was shopping in a local department store when I passed by a display table with this incredibly cool-looking product on it. It was a sleek, wallet-sized white case connected by audio wires to a set of speakers playing 70's disco music *(I loved the BeeGees)*. I walked over to the table and started interacting with what I now know to be an original iPod. I could not believe what I was seeing. An entire music library you could hold in the palm of your hand. Immediately I began a campaign to all of my friends and family regarding my need for an iPod. Cell phones had been gaining in popularity, but I did not see any upside to people being able to call me anytime they wanted, so I had no desire to purchase one. But the iPod was different. It spoke to my soul. I had to have it.

My Christmas gift from my youth group that year commenced a journey into technology that captivated my imagination. But it was Time Magazine's invention of the year not long afterwards that brought us face-to-face with maybe the most challenging parenting decision of our lives. What was this invention? It was Steve Jobs' and Apple's creation of the iPhone. This was not just a phone, but a small, internet-connected computer that could be kept in your pocket. I had been begrudgingly using a cell phone for a couple of years due to my executive position, but the iPhone was different. It looked awesome and it meant that with a cell connection, I could have instant access to any information on the internet I desired. In only a few short years the portable music library had transformed into the following comprehensive items: a phone, a camera, a photo library, a television, a movie theater, a book library, social media network, and the list goes on. This was a huge technological leap from my childhood of black and white television, only three channels and waiting on the white dot to become a full screen picture. Joining the technology express train has been a great ride. I have the latest cell phone, tablet and a laptop computer. But this multi-media revolution began taking place when our children were eleven, eight and five years old. We had a problem on our hands. At what level of involvement do we allow our children to participate partially or fully in this new technology? When an envoy from a distant land seeks to enter your home bearing gifts, you need wisdom from the Lord on how to respond. Wisdom is necessary because it gives parents the ability to navigate through our children's education, entertainment and relationship minefields.

Almost overnight, children and teenagers all around us began showing up with these new items. Every tween and teen we knew seemed to have access to these devices. As parents how were we supposed to navigate the cultural changes? Society dictates that our children can legally drive a car around the age of sixteen, vote and go to war at age eighteen and purchase alcohol when they are twenty-one years old. What is the legal age for a small item that can allow a child a new world of relationships outside of their parents' knowledge? When are our children old enough to make the right choices about the potentially dangerous information, images and people who might be hiding on the internet? We needed wisdom. We needed to understand the times. We needed to make sure we traveled the road best taken. What did we do? We sought the Lord and we felt like he gave us some answers. Michelle and I established phone, social media and internet guidelines for our children to follow. Our children had to wait until certain ages and levels of maturity before we would allow access to these new toys. Our decisions were based on what the Lord spoke to us. It is not necessary for me to share specific guidelines because this is not that type of book. It is not my place to tell when you should allow your child to have their own cell phone or what types of media choices you should make for them. But this is just one example of the many times you will be given the opportunity to walk on wisdom's road.

LEGACY > AMBITION

Hezekiah received the envoys from Babylon and proudly showed them all the treasures of his kingdom without any consideration of their ulterior motives. But his final error in parental judgement was the most tragic. Almost before the Babylonians had left the city, the prophet Isaiah appeared before Hezekiah once again. His question to the king got straight to the point. ***"What did those men say and where did they come from?" (II Kings 20:14)*** The king told him that they were from Babylon, a faraway land. The prophet asks a final question. ***"What did they see in your palace?" (vs. 15)*** Hezekiah's response displays his ignorance of what was at stake. ***"They saw everything in my palace...There is nothing among my treasures that I did not show them." (vs. 15)*** Isaiah thunders back a reply that starts with ***"Hear the word of the Lord..." (vs. 16)***

When a prophet starts a sentence with that phrase it usually is not good news for the hearer. The word of the Lord to Hezekiah was a sobering prophecy regarding the future of Judah. Isaiah told the king that one day the Babylonians would come and take all of the palace treasures to Babylon. He also told him that some of his future descendants would be taken into captivity as well. They would serve as eunuchs *(becoming a eunuch is painful to think about)* in a Babylonian king's palace. There was no good news in this message from the Lord.

Think back to the beginning of this chapter. When Isaiah gave Hezekiah the message that he was going to die, what did he do? He wept bitter tears and cried out to God for a miraculous healing. What does Hezekiah do or say when he receives a death sentence regarding his generational legacy? ***"The word of the Lord you have spoken is good," Hezekiah replied. For he thought, "Will there not be peace and security in my lifetime?" (II Kings 20:19)*** Where is the same desperate cry of deliverance for his descendants that he had for his own life? For some reason, this great king of the Old Testament, a man who trusted the Lord and had served him faithfully his entire life, was too wrapped up in own legacy. His own ambitions and goals far superseded his concern for his children, grandchildren and great-grandchildren. You can stop wondering why such a great godly king had such a wicked son. It is because Manasseh watched his father throughout his childhood focus on the kingdom and not on his family. It is possible to pursue your goals and dreams and still pass on your faith to your sons and daughters.

It is our God-given responsibility to leave a legacy of spiritual momentum for our children. The roads of business opportunities, romantic relationships and kingdom pursuits must be chosen with the spiritual well-being of our children in mind.

I knew that when I walked out into the backyard that day to cry out to God for direction that the spiritual legacy of Paul, David and Susanna could possibly be at stake. Paul had made it clear that he would never forgive me if I uprooted him from the only place he had ever called home. Our church, our school and our families provided such a relational and spiritual protection over their lives that I was not sure could not be replicated in our new location. But on the other hand, what about the call of God on my life? What about my dreams to do something great with my time on the earth? Could I do that serving as an armor bearer to my boss, pastor and mentor for my entire life?

I prayed for an hour and a half. Ten minutes were left before we had to leave. I know when the Lord speaks to me. Jesus says in John's gospel that his followers should, ***"Know his voice" (10:4).*** But on this day there was nothing from him. I was seemingly on my own in deciding which road to take. Michelle and I had made two previous moves early in our marriage to pursue God's call on our lives, but on both occasions I had received clear instruction from the Lord. This time it was like God was saying, "Tim, it's up to you." It was clear to me which road I wanted to take, but which road was the best?

In 49 B.C. Julius Caesar was returning to Rome with his conquering army. Roman generals were only allowed to lead an army in certain areas of their empire and the shallow, fifty mile long, Rubicon River was the boundary by which a general would have to disband his army and complete the trip to Rome as a private citizen. Caesar spent the night dining with his military commanders and there he coined the famous phrase, "the die is cast." The next morning he got up and took his army across the river. When he committed to this decision he was breaking Roman law, placing himself in opposition to the Roman Senate and starting a civil war. "Crossing the Rubicon" is the "point of no return." There was no turning back for Julius Caesar when he set his feet on the other side of that river. The rest, as we say, is history.

This is how I felt on that day so many years ago. No matter which choice I made there was no turning back. If I said no to these opportunities at this stage of my life, then I was most likely permanently forfeiting any chance to lead a church of significant size and influence. If I waited another five to ten years then my age window of visionary leadership at a new church would have passed. I had reached the Rubicon River, the place of no return, for my own personal dreams and goals.

Finally, I made a decision. I decided to go against the dream of more independence, more power and more money. I walked back into the house, called the other church and told them we were not coming. I chose the "road less traveled and it has made all the difference." My decision to remain at my home church in a serving position has been more rewarding than I ever thought possible. Would everything have been okay if I had decided to pursue my own dream? I do not think I will ever know the answer to that question. Absent a clear word from the Lord, I was not willing to put my legacy at risk. I do know that my children to this point in their lives have walked in the godly footsteps of those in our family lineage that have gone before them.

Hezekiah loved his own legacy more than he loved his family and it cost him Manasseh, his son, and the security of his kingdom a hundred years later. Roads chosen today have a tremendous rippling effect on future generations, both for good and for evil.

My grandparents and parents have left me something of value. They left me a spiritual heritage that has now extended to the fourth generation. I want to do the same for those coming after me, should the Lord tarry. I commit my life to caring as much about my descendants as I do myself. Choose legacy. It is the road best taken.

CHAPTER 8

THE BEST ADVICE

Let the wise listen and add to their understanding, and let the discerning get guidance--for understanding proverbs and parables, the sayings and riddles of the wise. The fear of the Lord is the beginning of knowledge, but fools despise wisdom and instruction.
(Proverbs 1:5-7)

"When a child turns 12, he should be kept in a barrel and fed through the bung (knot) hole, until he reaches 16...at which time you plug the bung (knot) hole."
(Mark Twain)

"In this house, the tail does not wag the dog."
(Paul Elmer Ferguson)

Children are a heritage from the Lord, offspring a reward from him. Like arrows in the hands of a warrior are children born in one's youth. Blessed is the man whose quiver is full of them.
(Psalm 127:3-5)

The clock struck midnight (actually it was 12:30 a.m.) and my carriage was about to turn into a pumpkin. I had violated my weekend curfew one too many times and my dad had warned me that if it happened again then I would be grounded. I sprinted out of my girlfriend's house, jumped into my Chevy Nova and began the fifteen mile journey home. Driving down the dark two lane road at an excessive speed gave me a few minutes to formulate a plan that would allow me to escape punishment. Approaching my house, I turned off my headlights, cut the engine and coasted silently to a stop behind my dad's car. My bedroom was at the front of the house facing the driveway. I carefully raised the window that was always unlocked. I crawled through the window and landed softly on my bed, convinced I had won another round in the never-ending father versus son battle for independence.

My victory was short-lived as I noticed there was a large shadow at the end of my bed. It was my dad. He had been sitting there in the dark, waiting for me to arrive. My dad always was, and still is, a man of few words. All he said was "Give me the keys." I dutifully fished the keys out of my pocket and handed them over to him. He got up from the bed, headed for the door and turned back to offer one last piece of advice right before I began my thirty day sentence without an automobile. "Son, when I say something, I mean it."

The best, most exhaustive, parenting advice in the Bible is found in the book of Proverbs. Solomon, full of God-given wisdom, uses the phrase, ***"my son,"*** twenty-two times throughout this book. Each time he uses this phrase he is telling us that these are the timeless truths that godly parents should impart to their sons and daughters. These proverbs he wrote down for his son were meant to be used for wise living. But they were also words of wisdom that he wanted to be passed from one generation to the next.

My mom and dad both came from parents who gave them the gift of a spiritual legacy. They took that gift and proceeded to pass it down to me and my three younger sisters. I was by far the most rebellious of my mom and dad's four children. But my sins were mostly confined to lying, pride and a bad attitude. My actions did not manifest themselves in the typical outward behavior of a teenage sinner. I was a virgin when I married in my mid-twenties. I have only had about four alcoholic drinks in my life and never tried drugs *(except Advil)*.

My sisters, on the other hand, served the Lord their whole lives and the troubles they caused my parents would not be enough to fill a coffee cup. I remember walking into Delisa's *(she's three years younger than me)* room to pick on her when she was in junior high, only to discover her listening to Evie *(an early contemporary Christian music artist)* while kneeling beside her bed in prayer. Their commitment to the Lord their entire lives resulted in a remarkable legacy. Three of us are involved in pastoral full-time ministry and my other sister, Cherie and her husband, Mike, are faithful leaders in our church.

Why am I telling you all of this Ferguson family history? Because my parents did something right. They have some parenting wisdom that others can learn from. Solomon expected his son to continue the legacy with his children by putting his wise sayings into action. My dad never set me down after my children were born and gave me wise parenting advice. He never wrote a book that recorded any fatherly proverbs. But what he did do was leave me with a legacy of sayings. Sayings like, "Son, when I say something, I mean it." Sayings such as, "Little boys should be seen and not heard" or "Do you think money grows on trees?" These phrases drove me crazy when I was a child. But I have discovered that these sayings of my father have become my "go to" parenting statements to my children over the last twenty-five years. I now know that each of these sayings have embedded nuggets of parenting advice within. My dad had about a dozen of these that I remember. But I am only going to talk about three of them. These sayings are rooted in parenting truths that can change what you believe and the way you interact with your children. In the final chapter of this book I am going to give you the best help I can. Straight from the mouth of my father. It is the best advice.

THE SKY IS THE LIMIT

This saying had a number of different variations. Sometimes it would be "you can do anything you put your mind to" or it might be "it's possible for a plain, yellow pumpkin to become a golden carriage." It was a parenting proverb designed to tell me that other voices were not allowed to define my spiritual destiny. Jesus recited this to his disciples when he told them, ***"With man this is impossible, but with God all things are possible" (Matthew 19:26).*** Gabriel spoke the same truth to Mary after she questioned his pregnancy prediction because she had never had sex with another man. He replied, ***"For nothing is impossible with God" (Luke 1:37).*** When my parents said, "The sky is the limit," they were opening up a whole world of possibilities for God to do something great in my life in spite of what the circumstances might otherwise be saying.

My dad's words came back to me with a resounding force when our son, David, was going through a difficult time adjusting to the educational demands of upper elementary school. In our minds Paul had been ready to join Mensa by the time he was in the first grade. David, on the other hand, struggled in almost every area from an early age. His head was bigger than his body and it would cause him to topple over every time he tried to sit up as an infant. He never learned how to crawl like other babies, but he did have this weird way of launching himself forward using some kind of leapfrog maneuver. He did not start walking until he was nearing the age of two and he certainly could did not recite the alphabet or memorize all the NFL or NBA team mascots.

Reading did not come naturally to him, but to make matters even worse, he was unable to write normally. By the time David was in the fourth grade, it was no longer possible to hide his inability to write legibly. Cursive writing was out of the question, but his printing was almost worse. It would be a lower case letter followed by two capital letters which would be followed by two more lower case letters and so on. Imagine a poorly printed word that went something like this, *"sUPerFICiaL."* Every word David printed was like this and the computer typing displayed here is much neater than his actual writing. Teachers would complain and threaten to not give him a passing grade because they could not read his assignments. I sat down with him and spent hours trying to teach him how to start a sentence with a capital letter followed by only lower-cased letters. My instructional methods failed miserably. Our time together each evening usually ended with me saying *(maybe yelling)*, "How hard can it be to write a single word?"

The situation reached a critical point when we tried to have him bring a computer to school so he could type out his classroom work. Unfortunately, at the time, our school did not allow elementary students to have personal computers on the campus. We met with his principal about the situation and she said that the school would allow him to carry a personal computer if we had him tested for dysgraphia. My reply, "What's dysgraphia?" Dysgraphia, come to find out, is a student having difficulty writing while doing school work. It affects a person's handwriting ability and his motor skills. "Just get a confirmed, written diagnosis that he has dysgraphia and he can bring his computer," was her response to us. Problem solved, right?

No, not really. Remember, my dad always told me that the sky was my limit. I told Michelle that I did not want David being labeled with a learning disability. Do not get me wrong. I knew that he had always had a problem with his motor skills. It is why he had struggled with sitting up, crawling and walking. I was not denying reality. I just did not want that to be the defining word spoken over his life. I knew that God could do the impossible.

Michelle and I turned to the book of Daniel for parental hope. I love this story of the great Old Testament prophet. Daniel and his friends are taken from their home in Judah into captivity by the Babylonians. They are teenagers who are forced to learn the language, literature and lifestyle of the Chaldeans. Their parents were most likely killed in the attack on Jerusalem and they are now placed in an impossible situation. They are going to be eunuchs in the king's palace with no hope for a prosperous future. But even though the facts said their situation was hopeless, the sky was the limit for them. They trusted in the Lord in regard to their diet and after ten days, they were found ten times better than the other young men who were being trained for the king's service. They were praised by the king and put on a fast track for government success. But my favorite scripture and the one we quoted and prayed over David was this, ***to these four young men God gave knowledge and understanding of all kinds of literature and learning (Daniel 1:17).*** If God could do it for Daniel, Hananiah, Meshael and Azariah, then he could do it for my son. This verse told me that God cared about the learning ability of his sons and daughters. The sky would be David's limit. We would not allow his educational future be defined by anyone's voice other than God's.

The turnaround did not happen overnight. But he slowly improved in all areas of his education. By the time he graduated from high school he was in the National Honor Society and in the top ten of his graduating class. His handwriting still lacks a little clarity, but David is on the dean's list at the university he is attending. He is a walking, educational miracle. Of our three children, David is by far our most educationally independent and responsible student. We do not have to look over his shoulder and impart self-discipline. God has given him a supernatural hunger and ability for knowledge and understanding. Who knows? Someday, he might be the first in our family to receive his doctorate. The sky is the limit for my son.

Parents, stop listening to those words of defeat over the life of your sons and daughters. Tell them the sky is the limit. Teach them that when God is involved anything is possible. I know firsthand about how difficult it can be to shake off the negative reports spoken over your children. But in the moments of doubt and despair let my dad's advice, which is really kingdom advice, come into your spirit and believe that the sky is the limit for your sons and daughters.

THIS WILL HURT ME YOU MORE
THAN IT DOES YOU

Those were the words that came out of my dad's mouth right before his belt came down upon my little bottom. I remember my young mind thinking, "Easy for you to say. I'm the one getting the spanking." Why was I on the receiving end of my dad's discipline? A few hours earlier I had been sitting behind a girl *(her name escapes me)* in Mrs. McBroom's second grade class. Her long pigtail kept dangling on my desk as her head bobbed up and down with excitement. A thought straight from the voice of the enemy entered my mind, "What would happen if I cut off her pigtail?" James says a **person is tempted when they are dragged away by their own evil desire and enticed. Then, after desire has conceived, it gives birth to sin; and sin, when it is full-grown, gives birth to death *(James 1:14-15).*** My seven year old mind conceived this desire and this desire gave birth to sin. I reached into my pencil box, took out my safety scissors and cut off her pigtail. I learned that day that a seven year old could commit full-grown sin. I also learned that sin gives birth to death. In my case, it was death to a pain-free life and death to my personal freedom.

I was sent to the principal's office where I received a spanking with the school's paddle. Then he sent me home for the rest of the day where my mom banished me to my room to await my dad's inevitable judgement. The wait was a cruel and unusual punishment in-and-of itself. This was not the era of modern parenting. Today, when a child or a teenager gets in trouble, the parent quite often comes down to the school or church to condemn authorities while rationalizing or excusing the actions of their beloved offspring. This was the late sixties. Getting in trouble at school meant getting in worse trouble at home. I knew another round of physical punishment was coming from my father. He would not go yell at the teacher or the principal for their lack of supervision. He would not argue that there was a mistaken identity or demand video evidence. Once he learned of my hair styling mischief, my life as I knew it would be over.

Finally, he arrived home and entered my room. He took off his belt, told me to bend over his knee and spoke those familiar words: "Son, this is going to hurt me more than it hurts you." Today, because I am a father of three children of my own, I have a clearer understanding of what my dad was trying to say. He was hurt more than me. My actions were a reflection of my mom and dad's parenting skills and caused them a tremendous amount of emotional pain and disappointment. What parent wants to come home from work only to be met with the out-of-control behavior of his or her child? Something had to be done. I needed discipline. The Bible says *if you are not disciplined—and everyone undergoes discipline— then you are not legitimate, not true sons and daughters at all (Hebrews 12:8).* So my dad assumed the responsibility of altering his son's destructive path. His legendary lament conveyed the message that he did not enjoying disciplining me, but he was willing to take the necessary steps in order to insure my prosperous future. It did hurt him more than me.

This is not an illustration meant to justify or condemn corporal punishment. I only relate this memory to you because it was one of the many times I can recall my father taking the time to try to change the course of my inappropriate behavior. Every parent or guardian needs to understand the importance of discipline which is meant to correct rebellion and the household rules which are put in place for your child's protection. It is very emotionally painful for any mother or father to discipline their child or to hold fast to enforcing a family rule. But if you lack the will or fortitude to carry through with these responsibilities, then you are setting yourself up for parenting failure.

My dad's statement about how disciplining me, hurt him was one of the best pieces of advice I have ever received in raising my own children. Analyzing this famous saying gave me insight in how to discipline my children and how to establish our household rules. Here is what I have learned from my dad about the "hurts me more than it does you" advice.

First, make sure your discipline and your rules are rooted in love. You are treading on dangerous ground anytime anger or satisfaction is your primary emotion during these moments. This why the apostle Paul says, *"Fathers, do not exasperate your children" (Ephesians 6:4).* Discipline without love leads to your sons and daughters ultimately turning their backs on your leadership and guidance.

I was easily angered by the behavior of my children in their early years. Maybe my biggest parenting mistake was the inability to distinguish an accident from intentional rebellion. I often reacted the same way over a glass of spilled milk versus a willful act of disobedience. How can you determine if you are not reacting in love? It is simple. Use my dad's test. Do you want your discipline to hurt your child more than you were hurt? Too many times as a parent I have failed this test.

A few years ago, before David got his driver's license, I took him to a birthday party for one of his friends. I knew that it would be after midnight when the party was over so I told him to call Paul to get a ride home. This created a problem, because no twenty-something older brother wants to act as a chauffeur for his younger sibling, especially on a Friday night. Later that evening, Paul called to vociferously complain about his unfair assignment. I ended the conversation with a typical threat to pull the funding for his car payment, phone bill, insurance, college tuition and any other financial support I could think of. Our conversation ended in anger, but he did agree to do what I asked. I turned over in bed and went to sleep. Sometime around one in the morning, we received the phone call that every parent dreads. It was Paul on the phone, his voice trembling, telling us that he and David were in a car accident. Paul was so upset that he could barely tell me what happened. After a few minutes, I got the address and enough information to know that they were badly shaken up, but physically okay. I got dressed, rushed to the car and drove to the accident.

Driving on the scene of your child's accident where police cars, fire trucks and emergency vehicles are filling the sky with their flashing lights is a surreal experience. I saw the mangled car and was filled with a flood of emotions. Getting out of my car, I saw Paul and David walking toward me. Now that I was assured that they were physically okay, my fear quickly turned into anger. After talking to an officer and seeing the wreck, I could clearly ascertain that Paul was at fault in the accident. When we finally climbed into my car to go home I was prepared to lower the boom on my oldest son. Suddenly in my spirit, I heard the Holy Spirit say, "It was an accident. Be grateful that they are alive."

My dad's advice came back to me. In this moment I needed to hurt more than Paul. He had received a legal discipline *(traffic ticket)* that would cost him financially. He clearly was struggling with the emotional trauma of a near death experience. He did not need me to pile on. He needed me to be a loving dad in that moment, not an ogre, allowing fear and anger to dictate my actions. Remember, **love covers a multitude of sins (I Peter 4:8).**

Secondly, your discipline and rules need to be flexible. Make sure that some of your discipline and family guidelines are a hill worth dying over. Too often our decisions in these areas have the unintentional consequences of fostering rebellion. Emotional, rash statements and a failure to understand the changing cultural environment can lead to unenforceable penalties. Hold your ground on sin issues, but be willing to consult Scripture and listen to the Holy Spirit when it comes to the gray areas.

Yelling, "You're grounded for life" or threatening to throw away all of their toys if they do not clean their room, are not quality discipline recipes *(I may or may not have said these words a few times).* Saying, "You can't date until you're forty" or constantly tracking the movements of your twenty-five year old son or daughter, are rules that are unreasonable. Be flexible. Be willing to adapt your parenting techniques to the age of your children and the changes in our society.

We had a rule when Paul and David were younger that they were not allowed to see Disney movies. I know you are thinking that we were unreasonable, overbearing parents. You are probably right. But again I counsel you not to judge us too harshly. There are probably some irrational rules *(no sugar or no fast food)* that you will be unable to enforce throughout your child's entire life. I did not think that watching a Disney movie was a sin. I just thought that some truths being taught in "Little Mermaid," "The Lion King" and "Aladdin" were not appropriate for our preschool children. Imagine my surprise when they started coming home from our Christian school after school care telling us all about the cool Disney movies that they were watching. Instead of ranting and raving at the leadership for corrupting the minds of my two sons I realized that I was going to have to flex a little to adapt to the culture around them. We still did not go to the theatre until they were in upper elementary *(Toy Story 2 was the first one)* or buy the popular children's movies for them to watch over and over again. But what we did do was try and teach our children to make quality, good worldview entertainment choices as they moved into their adolescent years.

What kind of parent would I be if I still tried to control their viewing habits? As they matured in wisdom and stature, we had to flex some of our family rules. Discipline has flexed from a plastic spoon to "let me have your car keys or your phone." But the principle remains the same. I do not want my punishment to hurt them to the point of exasperation. Michelle and I have established some boundaries that we have occasionally moved a little because we were causing too much pain in relating to their peers. These changes are always based in prayer and not in opposition the Word of God.

Finally, when it comes to establishing discipline, remember that "love is unconditional, but trust is earned." In spite of my dad's firm discipline, I never doubted his love for me. How did he know when to discipline? Anytime my rebellion violated his trust. My actions often caused a major withdrawal from my parents' trust account. But my dad instinctively knew how to administer a loving punishment that would be appropriate and would not cause me to be hurt more than my actions had hurt them.

A trust violation requires a parental response. Put their "you don't love me" protests aside and follow through with reasonable discipline. Just because you do not trust your child in certain areas for a season does not mean that you do not love them. Sometimes when I tell Paul, David or Susanna that they cannot have what they are asking for due to a trust failure, it does hurt me more than it does them. There is nothing I enjoy more than giving my children the desires of their heart. But there are conditions for our financial favor.

In closing this section, I could give you our guidelines for dating, movies, television, music, cell phone, the internet or college. But this is our family, based on what we believe God has spoken to us. The commandments are timeless, but some traditional practices of families are not. Be led by the Spirit. My dad's advice to make sure it hurts you more will always be a good starting point.

IN THIS HOUSE THE TAIL DOES NOT WAG THE DOG

In elementary school I learned that the galaxy we lived in was called the Milky Way. As part of that galaxy our solar system, consisted of the sun *(a star)* and the nine planets *(now there is only eight since Pluto has been demoted for some reason)* that orbited the sun. This science lesson taught me that the earth revolved around the sun. This was news to me because I had always assumed that our planet was the center of the universe. My teacher, Miss Angel, said that without the sun the world as we know it would cease to exist.

This concept of the sun being the center of our known existence is one that my dad co-opted to fit his parenting philosophy. He made it very clear that we were the planets and he and my mom were the sun. Thus the saying, "In this house, the tail doesn't wag the dog." Anytime one of my sisters or I would protest a family decision or activity choice, out would come this well-worn statement. Over the years, he came up with other stinging rebukes whenever I tried to assert my own authority over his. These new sayings basically carried the same meaning. Phrases like, "What part of no, do you not understand? Or "Last time I checked, no one died and made you the boss." No matter how hard I tried, I was never able to gain control over the work, church or recreational decisions of our home. Certainly, we were able to influence our parents at times, but there never was much doubt about who was in charge.

I have noticed a significant cultural shift in parenting philosophy over the last few years. In many homes, children are not the planets revolving around the lives of their parents, but parents have turned into the satellites orbiting their children, who have become the center of the family's universe. The list of examples I could cite is endless, but suffice it to say, if you are constantly making decisions based primarily on the desires of your offspring, then you are violating sound parental wisdom.

This societal change has resulted in the child being placed onto a pedestal that can almost be seen as worship. The Ten Commandments begin with the admonition to ***"Have no other gods before me" (Exodus 20:3).*** In the New Testament, the greatest commandment is defined as loving ***"The Lord your God with all your heart and with all your soul and with all your mind" (Matthew 22:37).*** Resist the temptation to make your son or daughter an object of worship. Children are instinctively brilliant at perceiving this potential weakness. If your tendency is to place their wishes above anything else, then they will take full advantage of the opportunity. Over time you will discover yourself being held captive to their demands. There are moments when it is necessary to say "in this house the tail does not wag the dog." Your child is not in charge. You are.

Of course we will make sacrifices on behalf of our children. But it should be based on God's wisdom, not because we are afraid of losing our status as the "cool" parent. My dad had no fear when it came to potentially losing "cool" points. If it meant I needed to be told no or taught a valuable life lesson, then he was willing to risk my temporary disfavor in order for this goal to be accomplished.

There is no better illustration from my childhood about this advice than my sixth grade city basketball championship game. There are three things to know about me during this stage of my life. I loved basketball more than life itself. I was good at basketball, the best player on my team. And I had a contemptuous attitude toward authority, especially referees. These three ingredients came together on a spring Saturday afternoon that resulted in one of my most traumatic childhood memories.

I was having the game of my life and late in third quarter of a very close game, I received my second technical foul for arguing a call with the referee *(even today, nothing challenges my walk with Lord like a bad call from a ref)*. My coach called a time out to calm me down and I looked up from the huddle to see my dad standing behind the bench. He called my coach's name and told him, "Tim's done." My coach, not fully understanding at first, slowly realized that I was no longer going to be an option as a player for the rest of the game. My dad came over to me and said, "Let's go sit in the stands." I was rebellious, had an attitude and a smart mouth. But I had a healthy fear of my father. It never occurred to me to disobey, but I did protest vehemently to no avail.

Sitting in the stands in the fourth quarter watching my dreams of a city championship slip away was more than I could bear. I kept pleading with my father to allow me to return to the game. "I've learned my lesson. I'll never do it again. Please, Dad." What kind of father embarrasses his son in front of his family, friends and the entire city? Did my dad not care about how this discipline would affect the rest of my life? What if I decided to hate him forever? With finality, my dad looked at me and said, "What part of no, do you not understand? You're not going back in." In other words: "In this house, the tail does not wag the dog." This decision by my dad would cost him my favor. For days afterwards, I treated him like he had the plague. The punishment did hurt him more than me, because not only was he unable to enjoy being the father of a basketball hero, but he also suffered my temporary wrath.

But because he refused to make me the center our family's solar system, I would learn a valuable lesson that has allowed the Holy Spirit to channel my fiery, competitive attitude into kingdom purposes *(for the most part)*. I urge you to take your place as the spiritual authority in your home. Be willing to stand by the difficult decisions that are in your child's best interests.

The journey to write this book began over nine months ago at the beginning of Susanna's senior year in high school. As I type these final words, her graduation day is less than forty-eight hours away. No longer do I have a child in my home to be their absolute authority. I now have three adults living with us as they approach the coming transition to their own families and homes. I am filled with joy at the young men and woman that they have become. But I know that this is not the end for Michelle and I. We will guide and pray with them over their relational and occupational futures. We will start all over soon with grandchildren. Fear still tries to come our way due to the unforeseen future. But the message at the end is still the same as it was at the beginning of this book.

Our three children are the best of us. We believe that the best is yet to come.

Printed in the United States
By Bookmasters